MEDIA, FEMINISM, CULTURAL STUDIES

Stepping Forward: Essays, Lectures and Interviews
by Wolfgang Iser

Genius and Loving It! Mel Brooks
by Thomas Christie

The Comic Art of Mel Brooks
by Maurice Yacowar

Marvelous Names
by P. Adams Sitney

Cixous, Irigaray, Kristeva: The Jouissance of French Feminism
by Kelly Ives

Jean-Luc Godard: The Passion of Cinema / Le Passion de Cinéma
by Jeremy Mark Robinson

Liv Tyler
by Thomas A. Christie

The Cinema of Richard Linklater
by Thomas A. Christie

John Hughes
by Thomas A. Christie

Walerian Borowczyk
by Jeremy Mark Robinson

The Art of Katsuhiro Otomo
by Jeremy Mark Robinson

Wild Zones: Pornography, Art and Feminism
by Kelly Ives

'Cosmo Woman': The World of Women's Magazines
by Oliver Whitehorne

Andrea Dworkin
by Jeremy Mark Robinson

The Erotic Object: Sexuality in Sculpture From Prehistory to the Present Day
by Susan Quinnell

Women in Pop Music
by Helen Challis

Julia Kristeva: Art, Love, Melancholy, Philosophy, Semiotics
by Kelly Ives

Luce Irigaray: Lips, Kissing, and the Politics of Sexual Difference
by Kelly Ives

Helene Cixous I Love You: The Jouissance *of Writing*
by Kelly Ives

Detonation Britain: Nuclear War in the UK
by Jeremy Mark Robinson

The Sacred Cinema of Andrei Tarkovsky
by Jeremy Mark Robinson

Akira: The Movie and the Manga
by Jeremy Mark Robinson

The Art of Masamune Shirow (3 vols)
by Jeremy Mark Robinson

FORTHCOMING BOOKS

Legend of the Overfiend
Death Note
Naruto
Bleach
Hellsing
Vampire Knight
Mushishi
One Piece
Nausicaä of the Valley of the Wind
The Twilight Saga
Harry Potter

TUPAC SHAKUR

SPIRITUALITY AND POLITICS

Tupac Shakur

SPIRITUALITY AND POLITICS

William Whalen

Crescent Moon

Crescent Moon Publishing
P.O. Box 1312, Maidstone
Kent, ME14 5XU, Great Britain
www.crmoon.com

First published 2023.
© William Whalen 2023.

Set in Times New Roman 10 on 14pt.
Designed by Radiance Graphics.

The right of William Whalen to be identified as the author of this book has been asserted generally in accordance with sections 77 and 78 of the Copyright, Designs and Patents Act 1988.

All rights reserved. No part of this book may be reprinted or reproduced, stored in a retrieval system, or transmitted, in any form or by any means, electronic, mechanical, photocopying, recording or otherwise, without permission from the publisher.

British Library Cataloguing in Publication data available for this title.

ISBN-13 9781861719096
ISBN-13 9781861719126

The publisher wishes to thank Steve Barrett.

CONTENTS

Tupac Timeline ✣ 11

Intro: Thug Bodhisattva ✣ 17

1 Tupac's Skand(h)as ✣ 48

2 Tupac's Sacred Biotech ✣ 84

3 Tupac and the Ecstasy of God ✣ 110

Bibliography ✣ 159

Dr William Whalen is an independent researcher who received his doctoral degree from the University of Albany in 2014. His dissertation focuses on how a handful of contemporary American authors speak back to and reappropriate sacred formulations of human bodies that figure individual human beings as having both masculine and feminine aspects. Chapters are dedicated to the artists Octavia Butler, Cormac McCarthy, Chuck Palahniuk, and rapper Lil Wayne.

While completing his dissertation, William Whalen taught as an adjunct at the University of Albany for seven years. His courses primarily focused on American literature, literary theory, and writing composition. Whalen has been a fan of Tupac Shakur since high school, but he first began closely studying and teaching Shakur when, as an undergraduate, he started a volunteer program to teach poetry and creative writing to inmates at Coxsackie Correctional Facility. His undergraduate honors dissertation was on Shakur, and he frequently included Shakur's works in the syllabi of the college courses he taught. Whalen is currently writing a book that uses Vajrayana Buddhism as a theoretical lens to analyze the lyrics, art, journals, and life of Kurt Cobain.

Author's warning: The subject matter researched herein is not for children or young adults.

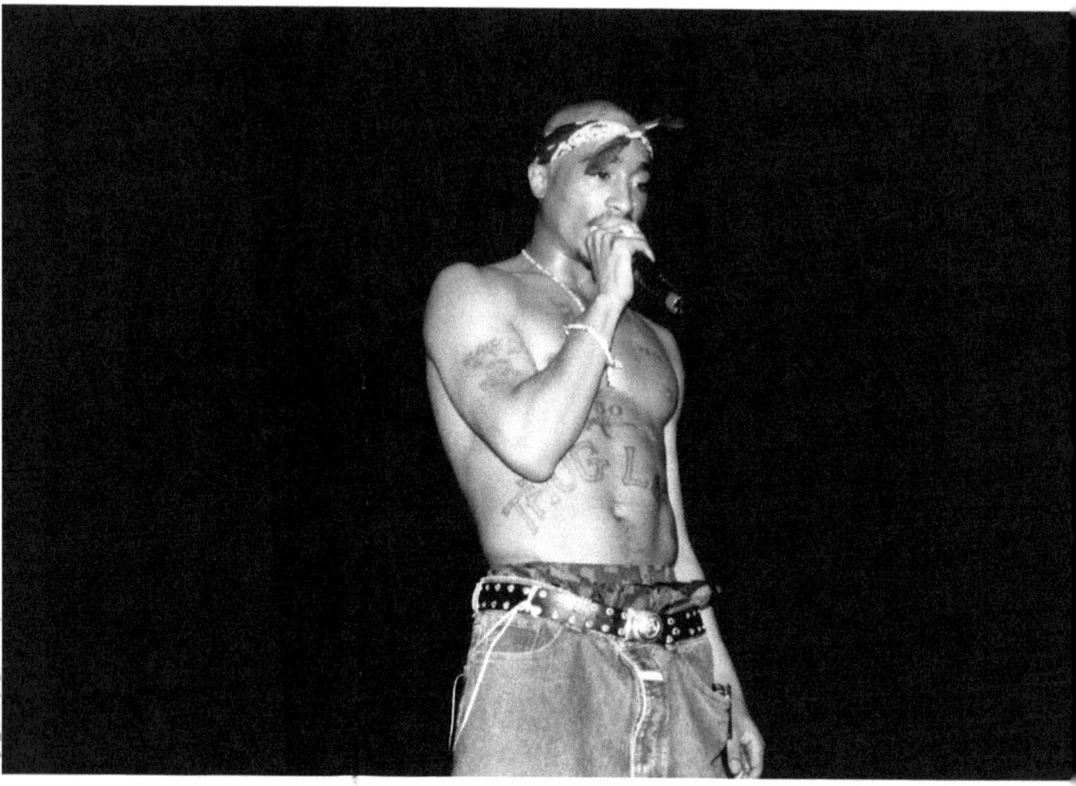

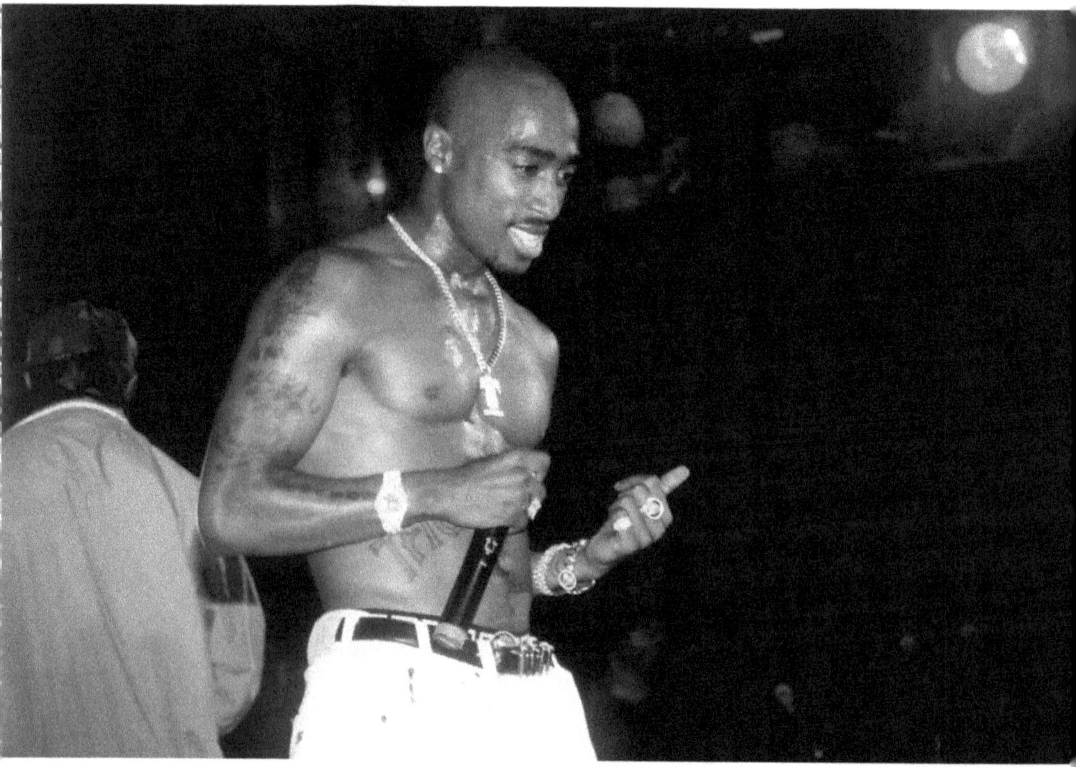

Tupac Timeline

- June 16, 1971. Lesane Parish Crooks (whose name would shortly after be changed to Tupac Amaru Shakur) is born to Black Panther activist Afeni Shakur only one month after she secured her own release from Manhattan's New York Women's House of Detention, where she and other Black Panthers were being charged with conspiracy to bomb police stations and other public buildings. Tupac is named after an Incan emperor who resisted Spanish rule and whose name means "intelligent warrior."

- 1973. Hip-hop is born (so most accounts say) at the legendary party DJ Kool Herc plays for his little sister in the Bronx, New York City.

- 1984. Afeni moves her family (Tupac and his little sister Sekyiwa) to Baltimore. Tupac enrolls at the Baltimore School for the Arts, where he studies ballet and Shakespeare, starts his first rap group, and befriends Jada Pinkett Smith. Afeni battles crack addiction. Tupac hustles to help make money.

- 1988. Afeni moves her family to Marin City, California, where Tupac meets Leila Steinberg, who will become his poetry teacher and first manager. Steinberg gets Tupac an audition as a roadie and backup dancer with the Digital Underground.

- Between 1990 and 1991, while touring with the Digital Underground, frontman Shock G lets Tupac begin to rap a little onstage. Tupac's appearance on the Digital Underground's 'Same Song' will be the start of his recording and professional career as a hip-hop artist.

- Interscope Records founder Ted Field gives his daughter a demo of *2Pacalypse Now*. She likes it, and so Tupac's debut album is released on November 12, 1991.

- October 17, 1991. Oakland police assault Tupac for jaywalking the same day his first solo video airs on *Yo! MTV Raps*.

- In April 1992, an 18-year-old shoots and kills a Texas state trooper during a traffic stop. He states he was inspired to shoot the officer because he was listening to *2Pacalypse Now*. Vice President Dan Quayle tries to get the album pulled from the shelves.

- In 1992, Tupac writes and presents a 26-point program called 'The Code of Thug Life' at a meeting of rival gangs, the Bloods and the Crips, to try and unite them. It was modeled on Black Panther Huey P. Newton's 'Ten-Point Program.' At a tattoo parlor in Houston the same year, Tupac receives his infamous Thug Life tattoo, which he later says is an acronym for 'The Hate U Gave Little Infants Fucks Everyone.'

- August 12, 1992. A 6-year-old is struck and killed by a stray bullet from Tupac's handgun, which Tupac pulls on a crowd who is angry with him about what he'd said concerning LA in a recent interview. After brandishing the weapon, Tupac accidentally drops the gun onto the ground, where it is recovered by his stepbrother Maurice Harding. It's unclear who pulled the trigger. Due to a lack of evidence, no criminal charges are filed. $500,000 is later paid in a wrongful death suit.

- Tupac has a starring role in the 1992 film *Juice*.

- February 1993. Tupac releases his second studio album, *Strictly 4*

My N.I.G.G.A.Z.

• In 1993, Tupac is fired from his role in the Hughes brothers' film *Menace II Society* for being disruptive on set. Not long after, he spends 15 days in jail for assaulting Allen Hughes and then bragging about it on *Yo! MTV Raps*.

• Also in 1993, Tupac stars in the film *Poetic Justice* alongside Janet Jackson.

• October 1993. Tupac is charged with shooting two off-duty police officers, one in the abdomen and the other in the buttocks. A road rage incident erupts when the off-duty officers claim they were almost hit by a vehicle crossing the street with their wives. Tupac is in the second car and is, from his point of view, defending his friends. It's disputed who shot first. Charges are dropped when one of the officers later discloses that the gun he used in the shootout was taken from the evidence room. One of the officers wins a $2 million default judgment from Tupac's estate in 1998.

• November 1993. Tupac is charged with sodomy and sexual assault.

• October 1994. *Thug Life Vol. 1*, the only album Tupac records as a member of the rap group Thug Life, is released.

• November 1994, one day before Tupac's sexual assault trial, three men rob and shoot Tupac five times at a recording studio not far from Times Square. Famously, Tupac believes this robbery and shooting is orchestrated by Sean "Puffy" Combs and his once-friend Christopher Wallace, also known as Biggie Smalls. Tupac is acquitted on the sodomy accounts the next day but is found guilty of sexual abuse for 'forcibly touching the woman's buttocks.'

• Also in 1994, Tupac appears in the sports-crime film *Above The*

Rim, the last film he's in to be released in his lifetime. *Bullet*, *Gridlock'd*, and *Gang Related* will all come out posthumously.

• February 1995. Tupac is sentenced to four and a half years in prison for sexual abuse but gets released on October 12, 1995. Following his release, he tells *VIBE* magazine that he feels ashamed for not protecting the women. 'I feel ashamed because I wanted to be accepted. I didn't want no harm done to me. I didn't say anything.'

• March 1995. Tupac releases his third studio album, *Me Against The World*.

• October 1995. Suge Knight pays Tupac's $1.4 million bail. Tupac signs with Death Row Records.

• February 1996. Tupac releases *All Eyez On Me* (the last album to be released in his lifetime).

• September 7, 1996. Tupac is shot to death while riding in a BMW with Suge Knight in Las Vegas.

• November 1996. Tupac's *The Don Killuminati: The 7 Day Theory* is posthumously released.

• In 1997, Afeni starts the Tupac Amaru Shakur Foundation, whose mission is 'To address mental health conditions and eradicate the effects of trauma on our community by providing access to therapeutic resources, creative arts, and education designed to support mental health, physical wellness, and overall development.' Tupac's sister, Sekyiwa, runs the foundation following Afeni's death.

• November 1997. Tupac's *R U Still Down? (Remember Me)* is posthumously released.

• December 1999. Tupac's album with the Outlawz, *Still I Rise,* is posthumously released.

- March 2001. *Until The End Of Time* is posthumously released.

- November 2002. *Better Dayz* is posthumously released.

- December 2004. *Loyal To the Game* is posthumously released.

- November 2006. *Pac's Life* is posthumously released.

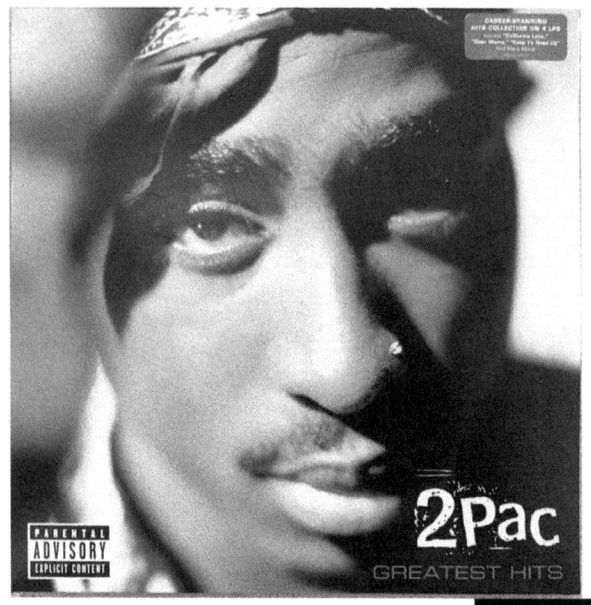

Tupac Shakur, album covers.

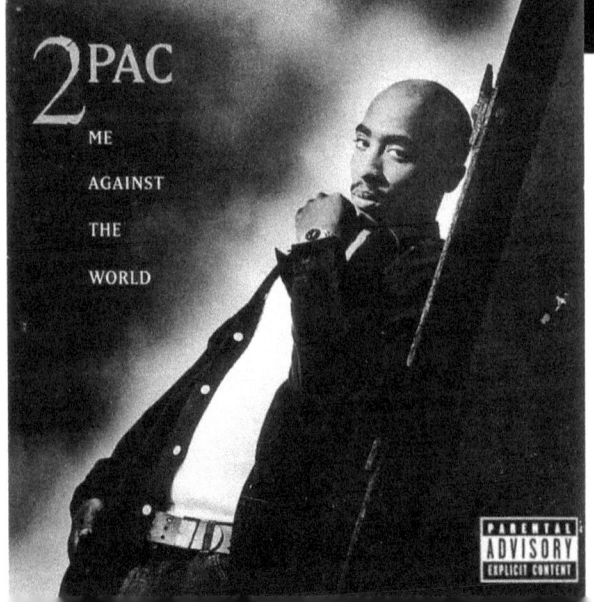

Intro

Thug Bodhisattva

'All warfare is based on deception. Hence, when able to attack, we must seem unable; when using our forces, we must seem inactive; when we are near, we must make the enemy believe we are far away; when far away, we must make him believe we are near... Attack him where he is unprepared, appear where you are not expected.'

Sun Tsu, *The Art of War*

In an interview featured in the documentary *Tupac Shakur: Before I Wake*, hip-hop superstar Tupac says, 'My inner peace is knowing that once everybody takes the time to really see what type of person I am, they'll be surprised.' Tupac Shakur – in his mind and the minds of many of his students and fans – is enlightened, converted, or twice-born. In a 1994 interview with Ed Gordon, Tupac states that he 'went through a metamorphosis' and that he's 'doing God's work' because 'God has cursed' him 'to see what life should be like.' Tupac saw himself as an awakened Buddha, who, following in the footsteps of Thomas à Kempis' *Imitation of Christ* (a book we know Tupac read), finds Christ within. This is echoed in the song titled 'R U Still Down? (Remember Me),' where, according to some accounts, we're pressed to recall both that the Buddha's last words on this Earth were 'Remember me as the one who woke up' and that during Christ's last supper with his Apostles, before instructing them in the enigmatic ritual of consuming his body and blood, Jesus says, 'Do this in remembrance of me.'

The purpose of this work is to interpret and analyze some of the more encrypted esotericisms at play in the lyrics and practice of Tupac Shakur, as well as consider their political implications to attempt to come to a better understanding of Tupac's spirituality and why he felt the world could benefit from his teachings. Like Christ, who repeatedly says, 'He who hath ears to hear, let him hear,' Tupac says in various ways, 'Holler if ya hear me,' suggesting that his words are not only literal but also require deep interpretive consideration. In an interview at Clinton Correctional Facility in 1995, Tupac states, 'My music is spiritual, if you listen to it. It's all about emotion. It's all about life... I tell my innermost, darkest secrets. I reveal myself in every one of my records.' This work will look deeper into what spirituality looks like for Tupac and not only what his music implies about his spiritual ideas but also what they suggest about his spiritual practices.

Much has been written about Tupac Shakur, who died in 1996, and several documentaries and a Hollywood film are dedicated to telling his story. Even though that story has been told and retold, it is important to highlight that various filmmakers and biographers choose to emphasize different aspects of Tupac's epic journey from a sensitive young man heavily involved in the arts – dance, theater, and writing – to the weed-smoking, gun-toting, gangster rapper who at the age of 25 is gunned down on the streets of Las Vegas following a Mike Tyson boxing match. How Tupac's story is framed and what aspects are focused on significantly impact how he is understood. Everyone who tells a version of Tupac's story seems to recognize an inextricable link between Tupac and whatever he refers to in the many instances he evokes 'the sacred' or the name of 'God,' but hardly anyone has even scratched the surface to begin boring into the depths of his complex, sometimes paradoxical spirituality.

Michael Eric Dyson is the only biographer and intellectual to really get the ball rolling for serious inquiry into the philosophical and spiritual lyrics of Tupac Shakur. This is largely because Dyson, in his innovative work *Holler If You Hear Me: Searching for Tupac Shakur*, makes an appropriately big deal out of Tupac's relationship with his poetry teacher, first producer, and 'literary soul mate' Leila Steinberg. Dyson not only organizes the entire chapter on Tupac's extraordinary education around Steinberg but also places Steinberg, her relationship with Tupac, and her insight into how he is to be interpreted front and center for his chapter on Tupac's spirituality. In "No Malcolm X in My History Text," the chapter named after lyrics from 'Words of Wisdom,' a track off Tupac's first album, *2pacalypse Now*, Steinberg shares with Dyson the reeling extent to which Tupac was obsessed with reading and knowledge.

As a 17-year-old recently relocated to Marin City, California, from Baltimore, Maryland, Tupac moved in with Steinberg, her husband, and their children after meeting her through a mutual friend and attending her writing and performance workshop. When Steinberg and Shakur met, Tupac, unable to further tolerate his mother, who was suffering from drug addiction, was living on the streets. Before becoming his first hip-hop manager, Steinberg convinced Tupac to join her in volunteering with the organization Young Imaginations, where Steinberg lectured to help educate 'children about history, culture, and politics' and Tupac, once on board, rapped. Dyson underscores, however, that, while living with Steinberg, Tupac and her spent most of their time together 'reading books at their favorite haunt, L.A.'s Bohdi Tree Bookstore.' And this was the crux of their relationship. They were, as Dyson emphasizes, 'literary soul mates.' Even after Steinberg ceased to manage Tupac's rap career, the two remained close friends and study companions. While interviewing Steinberg for *Holler If You Hear Me*, Dyson was invited to Steinberg's home to view some of the books she kept from Tupac's collection after he passed. Tupac read a variety of works on race, class, and gender, but he also read an impressive number of texts on philosophy, psychology, and especially spirituality, which is the primary focus of our inquiry. Some of the works Tupac read include books on anarchy and Platonism, Khalil Gibran, *Zen and the Art of Motorcycle Maintenance*, an anthology of Friedrich Nietzsche, books by Sigmund Freud and Carl Jung, Sun Tzu's *The Art of War*, Jack Kornfield's *Teachings of the Buddha*, St. John of the Cross and *The Cloud of Unknowing*, Gershem Scholem's edition of the *Kabbalah*, the *Bhagavad Gita*, and *The Tibetan Book of the Dead*.

In Dyson's chapter on Tupac's spirituality titled "But Do the Lord Care?," taken from lyrics off the track 'Only God Can Judge Me' from *All Eyes on Me*, Dyson claims, 'Tupac was obsessed with God.' Dyson also states that, according to Steinberg (whom Dyson quotes throughout the chapter), Tupac 'yearned as a youth to create a society where spiritual enlightenment could be fostered and respected.' In Dyson's words, Tupac 'aimed to enhance awareness of the divine, of spiritual reality, by means of challenging orthodox beliefs and traditional religious practices.' This includes Tupac's belief that revolution not only has to be 'spiritual' but also, as Dyson quotes Steinberg, has to embrace the 'physical, sexual, and political.' As though to suggest that Tupac never got around to fulfilling the wishes of his youth regarding his political spirituality, the above quote emphasizes Dyson's distinction between the young Tupac who studied sacred life and the more mature Tupac who became an outspoken proponent of what Tupac called 'thug life.' Dyson punches this distinction again when he says 'the *younger* Tupac entertained a holistic view of social change that did not downplay the crucial role of spirituality...' by building on Steinberg's important statement that Tupac

> thought that spirituality... is racially biased... [because it is] a privilege to be able to ponder the great spiritual truths... And Pac wanted to open the doors for all of us to be able to have spiritual conversations and ponder the meaning of life.

Dyson further clarifies and adds nuance to his distinction between the young and mature Tupac when he admits that 'Tupac's passion for spiritual matters never left him, although its form and function in his later life may have become almost unrecognizable by earlier standards.' It is this 'unrecognizable' dimension of highly political spirituality in Tupac's lyrics that most concern us here.

In the documentary *Tupac Shakur: Thug Angel (The Life of an Outlaw)*, after sharing with viewers many of the sacred texts and intellectual interests of Tupac quoted above from Dyson's work, Leila Steinberg says, 'as you study Tupac's lyrics, you start to know and understand how much he incorporated his reading [into them]. Even his last albums.'

Steinberg's position is markedly different from Dyson's stance that spirituality in the lyrics of the mature rap icon Tupac Shakur are virtually unrecognizable. The way Dyson perceives it, as Tupac matures, something of his spirituality gets lost, while Steinberg sees it otherwise. She argues that nothing is lost '[e]ven in his last albums' and implies that Tupac's spirituality is then just packaged differently if not deliberately hidden. Tupac's spirituality, for Steinberg, remains in his mature works and is present for readers to unveil through close reading.

To be fair to the brilliant Michael Eric Dyson, he does labor a great deal in "But Do the Lord Care?" to highlight what he argues is Tupac's mature spiritual position, which he suggests is grounded in theodicy:

> [Tupac's] relationship to God during his rap career took the form of an ongoing argument about the suffering he saw and the evil he endured and expressed. The compassion he summoned as well as the raps he wrote were meant to expose and relieve the pain he witnessed. In traditional theological circles, the branch of thought that seeks to answer the unmerited suffering of believers is termed theodicy. It has an analogue in social science as well, where theodicy is concerned with discerning meaning in the suffering of the masses.

In addition to being an excellent biography of Tupac, Dyson's *Holler If You Hear Me* offers a thorough account of Tupac's dialog with God about the suffering of people in general, black people more closely, and, even most specifically, Tupac himself. Dyson's work comes out of the social sciences, and it is fundamentally a biography about Tupac and his social-justice politics as the son of a Black Panther trying to build on and modify the shortcomings of the '60s Black Power movement that animated but ultimately failed his mother, Afeni Shakur.

Steinberg, for us, is the key to opening up another spiritual dimension of Tupac, a dimension Dyson begins to show but doesn't unfold satisfactorily. Where Dyson knows sociology, we have our Ph.D. in literary analysis and have studied, like Tupac, *Kabbalah*, Kahlil Gibran, the *Tibetan Book of the Dead*, Freud, Jung, the *Bhagavad Gita*, and most of the other works Tupac read plus many more sacred texts he was likely exposed to in some way, shape, or form. So we begin our inquiry with Steinberg's hypothesis that Tupac has a deep spiritual dimension that can be ascertained through close literary analysis. The question we ask ourselves to start our inquiry, then, is why the esotericism? Why does Tupac hide his spirituality? If he wants to express something about the divine, why not just be explicit? And as soon as we ask this, we have to give pause for a moment, remembering the important work of Dyson insofar as it so poignantly tracks the multitude of instances in Tupac where he does explicitly express his faith, whatever that might mean to Tupac, instances like the track 'Who Do You Believe In,' where he overtly says 'Who do you believe in? I put my faith in God.' What we are really asking, then, isn't why does Tupac hide his spirituality (because he doesn't necessarily hide it), but is, instead, why is he explicit about it at times while at other times he conceals it?

These are the questions we have to ask if we take Steinberg seriously because what we understand her to be saying is that there is a spiritual dimension to all of Tupac's lyrics, meaning that there is even a spiritual dimension to all the business about 'bitches' and 'guns' and 'weed' and so forth, and not just in those obvious moments when Tupac dialogs with God to either praise Him or question Him as to why so much suffering has to occur. If we don't take Steinberg seriously but still analyze the profane in Tupac in search of deeper meaning, we wind up in the place where Dyson arrives (along with many other listeners, we're sure), which is that Tupac is conflicted, meaning something like – when Tupac dialogs with God he yearns for a holy life, but when he talks about and lives a life that involves guns and drugs, he is a sinner, and he is always trying to reconcile these conflicting aspects of his personality. What's more, it's not that we are disclosing Dyson's position; it seems clear that he is conflicted and that there are at least two Tupacs within Tupac. We aren't interested in suggesting that Dyson is false and Steinberg is correct, but rather, in exploring multiple truths by looking into the possibility that Tupac is always talking about God, as Steinberg suggests, but in a veiled way – this is especially true regarding his internal conflict, which we argue isn't a conflict between the sacred and unsacred but is instead just a sacred conflict. Unlike Dyson, who wrote an entire book expressing his interpretation of Tupac, Steinberg leaves us only with a little nugget of insight that goes unexplored, which we intend to begin to break apart here.

Let's elaborate on the idea that there are 'two Tupacs' within Tupac and also self-reflexively address the 'we' who is the author of this work. During an *Arsenio Hall Show* interview, Arsenio rightly states that Tupac doesn't present himself as a singular subject or individual but instead as a split person:

> Arsenio: See, I get a feeling there are two Tupacs. See, I mean, you're this kind, sensitive, friendly guy...
>
> Tupac: Friendly smelling guy [We assume that Tupac is addressing how he smells like marijuana].
>
> Arsenio: Yet you're involved in so much controversy...

For Arsenio Hall, Tupac is not one but two. Additionally, Tupac spells his name '2Pac,' not 'Tupac,' on his *All Eyez On Me* album, suggesting that he sees himself not as singular but as multiple. This point is furthered on the opening track of that album, 'Ambitionz Az a Ridah,' when Tupac says, 'My murderous lyrics equipped with the spirits of the Thugs before me.' Furthermore, in Dyson's chapter on Tupac's tattoos – "I Got Your Name Tattooed on My Arm" – Dyson interviews Tupac's friend Cassandra Butcher, who recalls Tupac's ruminations on his tattoo that reads '50 Niggaz' atop an image of an AK-47: 'I said, 'What does it mean?' He said, 'This means when you come up against me, it's like coming up against fifty niggas, because I've got the souls of all my brothers in me.'' Moreover, in one of his last interviews with *OKEJ* magazine, Tupac states that one of the biggest misunderstandings about him is that he's a one-sided individual:

> I'm a Gemini, young, black, gangsta but I've got many different sides, I'm about the community, I'm hungry for knowledge, I'm hard to put in a category, so that ones that try, just say I'm krazy.

In the spirit of Tupac's self-conceptualization, not as an individual but as a multitude, we too perceive ourselves as at least two, if not several, or a crowd. Tupac's philosophical position on identity, from which we take our cue, will become more apparent as we analyze his work.

There are a multitude of reasons why Tupac chooses to conceal his spirituality in his otherwise overt gangster rap lyrics. In an interview aired on the Urban Movie Channel following the 2017 release of the Shakur biopic *All Eyez On Me*, Leila Steinberg describes Tupac's lyrics as 'a code. A way to fight for freedom without those who weren't supposed to know knowing.' In *Holler If You Hear Me*, Dyson quotes Tupac, alluding to the notion of 'doublespeak' coming out of George Orwell's *1984*. 'Doublespeak' refers to deceptive language reversals and wordplay meant to ideologically shore up the ruling totalitarian government by covering over the violence that allows its systems and routines to function smoothly. For example, in *1984*, talking about the names of the branches or ministries of government and what they do, the text states, 'The Ministry of Peace concerns itself with war, the Ministry of Truth with lies, the Ministry of Love with torture and the Ministry of Plenty with starvation.' So by combining Steinberg's statement that Tupac's lyrics contain a hidden code intended only for the ears of the revolutionarily spiritual avant-garde with Dyson's documentation of Tupac's awareness of Orwell's concept of doublespeak, we hypothesize that, in his lyrics, Tupac develops a reverse kind of doublespeak that turns the Orwellian concept on its head and even forces listeners to recall that when Christ returns in *The Book of Revelation* he has a double-edged sword for a tongue.

It's possible that Tupac uses doublespeak not to sugarcoat gangsterism (which we're treating as a kind of microcosmic totalitarianism) but to disseminate revolutionary spirituality packaged as gangsterism. The question, then, is why would he do this? There could be a few reasons. As Steinberg already suggests, one reason might be to hide spiritual weapons of resistance from the oppressor. Another, ironically, might be to equip a potential oppressor with spiritual tools of resistance to prevent them from becoming an oppressor. Spirituality, especially the kind of unorthodox, esoteric arts Tupac would have been familiar with in Hinduism, Buddhism, *Kabbalah*, and Christian mysticism, all involve, in some manner, a war that is waged not only against evil without but, first and foremost, against the evil potential of the monopolistic ego within. By selling a way of life packaged as gangsterism (masculinity, conquest, competition, tribalism), especially to the externally and internally oppressed black youth of America suffering under the iniquities of a racist nation-state operating in service of the beneficiaries of global capitalism, and then stuffing that package full of the wherewithal necessary not only to destroy gangsterism without but to attack it at its egocentric core within, Tupac, we argue, plays a dangerous game, a game designed to attack and liberate his listeners simultaneously. It's by using his ego that Tupac is able not only to overcome his own egocentrism but to attack it in others. In 'All About U,' for example, it's clear that Tupac keeps secrets and plays dangerous games that he considers spiritual:

> Wise decisions, based on lies we livin'
> Scandalous times, this game's like my religion.

This deceptive and religiously scandalous game Tupac plays to liberate his fans would have certainly jeopardized his life if anyone who was seriously troubled were to find out what he was up to and blame Tupac for their problems instead of taking ownership of their own quest to transcend them.

In many spiritual disciplines, especially in the East, if one wants to study under a guru, one has to spend a tremendous amount of time proving to the guru that one is worthy because a true spiritual path is fraught with dangers at every turn. Christ, the Buddha, Osiris (pick your hero) – they all more or less go through hell before they get to heaven, and every serious spiritual master knows that some students go to hell, get stuck, and never make it out; meaning they wind up harming themselves or others. Even among those who do make it through, many struggle with horrible melancholy once they have to figure out how to reintegrate themselves into the ordinary everyday world.

According to theologian and philosopher Alan Watts, famous for teaching the West about Buddhism as well as bridging the gap between Eastern and Western religions, gurus also historically give their students a hard time based on the assumption that many students psychically reject the idea that enlightenment can come easy and so desire a grueling process leading up to deep spiritual understanding:

> So then, when you're in the way of waking up and finding out who you really are, you meet a character called a guru; as the Hindus say, this word, 'the teacher,' 'the awakener.' And what is the function of a guru? He's the man who looks at you in the eye and says, 'Oh, come off it! I know who you are... Basically, go right down to it. You're looking at me, you're looking out, and you're unaware of what's behind your eyes. Go back in and find out who you are...' There are all sorts of tricks, of course, that gurus play. They say, 'Well, we're going to put you through the mill.' And the reason they do that is, simply, that you won't wake up until you feel you've paid a price for it. In other words, the sense of guilt that one has, or the sense of anxiety, is simply the way one experiences keeping the game of disguise going on... You feel awful that you exist at all. But that sense, that sense of guilt, is the veil across the sanctuary... Why? Because you're saying to yourself, 'I won't wake up until I feel I deserve it...' So I invent for myself an elaborate system of delaying my waking up. I put myself through this test, and that test, and when I feel it's been sufficiently arduous, *then* I may at last admit to myself who I really am, and draw aside the veil, and realize that – after all, when all is said and done – I am that I am, which is the name of God.

For Watts, the guru only withholds his wisdom to parody the initiate's internalized repression. Reflecting back on them their own desire to hide things from themselves, the guru not only plays the role of the student's own internal policing apparatus but mocks them in the process of their quest to overcome themselves. This mockery, among other things, is intended to scare off those not prepared to deal with the humility and discipline required for the path to enlightenment while simultaneously helping those students who are ready to disinvest in their teacher's authority and become more self-reliant.

In his seminal work *The Phenomenology of Spirit*, 19th-century German philosopher Georg Wilhelm Hegel, the infamous apologist for racist colonialism, argues that a bondsman or slave will remain and is justified in remaining enslaved by a master up until the point that the slave himself realizes he's free and fights for his freedom. Appropriately for our topic here, it is unclear to philosophy scholars whether Hegel is talking about a kind of internal self-enslavement, an external form of enslavement between one person or group of people and another, or both simultaneously. This position isn't dissimilar from that of the guru of the East; until the student realizes that he and not his teacher is his primary source of knowledge and authority, it's fair game for the teacher to mock the student for investing in the teacher and not in himself.

Ironically, we can locate Tupac occupying a similar pedagogical position to that of the Eastern guru and Hegel. One critical difference that must be highlighted, however, is that with the Eastern guru and Tupac, we know neither is in any way justifying actual enslavement, which is at best unclear with Hegel, who quite possibly made the tragic mistake of assuming that what's true of one's inner world is always also true of the external world. Moreover, a critical distinction between Tupac and the Eastern guru must be highlighted: Tupac, unlike the Eastern guru, doesn't position himself as the teacher waiting for students to come to him in search of enlightenment. He instead actively hunts for them through his lyrics. This would mean that, like Watts' guru, who mimics and parodies the student's own internal repression, the violence Tupac performs is a violence that is not only aimed at liberating its so-called victim but one that personifies and reflects the inner conflict taking place within his listeners. Thereby, Tupac, at times, personifies the unconscious potential one has alienated from oneself – a potential that because it is alienated becomes 'demonic' – and, at other times, he personifies the hero aspect of self who is determined to master that alienated potential.

There is a similar practice to that of the taunting Eastern guru in African American culture. It's called the 'Dirty Dozens,' and, in its hip-hop configuration, it's much more 'Zen' than it is typically received. It's our position that Tupac not only draws from the Dirty Dozens but also blends his knowledge of Eastern gurus with it. In *The Signifying Monkey: A Theory of African American Literary Criticism*, American literary critic Henry Louis Gates Jr.'s seminal work on black vernacular, Gates analyzes Clarence Major's *Dictionary of Afro-American Slang* to clarify the definition of the 'Dirty Dozens':

> The 'Dirty Dozens' he defines as 'a very elaborate game traditionally played by black boys, in which participants insult each other's relatives, especially their mothers. The object of the game is to test emotional strength. The first person to give in to anger is the loser.'... For Major,

then, to Signify [or play the Dirty Dozens] is to be engaged in a highly motivated rhetorical act, aimed at figurative, ritual insult.

According to Gates' account of the Dozens, participants willingly play a game where they know they'll be intimately insulted, and they do this to achieve 'emotional strength.' By this, we believe Gates means that by building a tolerance or even numbness to verbal assaults, participants will free themselves of another's psychological power and control over them. But we argue there's more to the Dozens, which can be seen in Tupac's lyrics.

The Dozens is a simultaneously self-imposed and community-directed attack on a participant's ego. The 'first person to give in to anger,' then, isn't only 'the loser' because they've allowed another to determine how they feel and act – the first person to give in to anger is a loser because they failed to see themselves as a living and changing cluster of familial, historical, communal, and environmental cross-connections. The one to give into anger loses because he allows his mind to perceive itself as a single entity. In other words, he allows himself to see himself as an individual. The winner can come up with the quickest, wittiest comebacks simply because he neither perceives himself as a single self nor his opponent as a separate entity. Because he already sees his ego as a fake separation from his True Self, the one who is able to win wins because he directs his insults both against the other without but also, and most importantly, against his own ego-self within, and the winner's insults are so linguistically crafty because he formulates them in a polysemic way. On the surface, they appear to be directed at another, but, upon closer investigation, it becomes clear that they can also be interpreted to refer to oneself, and the ultimate impasse of the master Dozens practitioner is that the listener can never really tell whether it's one way, the other, or both. What's more, because the insults can be interpreted as self-reflexive, the listener is pulled into a similar loop of self-reflexivity, so that every insult can read as though it's directed at the listener, and, in a way, it is. Because the ego is not only the particular 'I' but is also the universal 'I,' an attack against one's ego is an attack against the ego in all.

Ram Dass (Richard Alpert) is a clinical psychologist and former advocate for psychedelics turned spiritual teacher, and, in one of his many famous lectures, he describes what novelist Hermann Hesse calls 'the game' in a way that is strikingly similar to our understanding of the Dozens:

> When we're talking about real freedom, we're talking about the freedom of awareness from identification with thought. That's the deepest kind of freedom the Buddha talks about, and so the exercise becomes – how do you live in form, how do you live your life and do everything you do everyday without getting lost in it so that you are in it but not of it, so that there is all the feelings and emotions and the play, but it has the quality of play? Hermann Hesse talks about it as 'the game' or a dance... The dance of life. The play or the dance. And how do you live your life in such a way that it's dance or play?

It's important to mark that spiritual thinkers Ram Dass and Hermann Hesse also thought of this practice of not identifying with one's ego-self as 'the game' because we argue that Tupac too conceptualizes his praxis in these terms. Tupac's caveat is that his 'game,' similar to the Dirty Dozens, utilizes ego to go to war both with the ego within and with other people's egos without. In this way, Tupac's method comes very close to certain esoteric approaches from the Vajrayana Buddhist tradition. In the *Hevajra Tantra*, for example, to move beyond the prison of duality, practitioners are told, 'You should kill living beings, speak lying words, take what is not given, consort with the women of others.' These words, we argue, as many others do, are to be taken figuratively, which isn't to say that the stakes are decreased. They are designed at every turn to attack the ego and its propensity toward property ownership over both self and others. The game of attacking the notion of ownership is, in our understanding, a huge aspect of what Tupac refers to when he mentions, as he often does, 'thug life'.

It's well known that Tupac made an acronym out of the phrase 'thug life': 'the hate you gave little infants fucks everyone.' Tupac even designed a program named Thug Life, intended to decrease violence between rival gangs and redirect their focus to empower black communities. However, we argue that, for Tupac, there is more to the term. In a 1994 interview with Benjamin Svetkey, Tupac states, 'I believe that God wants me to do something and it has to do with Thug Life.' Knowing what we already know about Tupac's saturation in the sacred texts of the East and Christian mysticism, as well as his lifelong exposure to circles of people exploring unorthodox spirituality, it's more than possible to consider that somewhere along his studies, Tupac became aware of the actual historical Hindi cult of thieves known as 'thuggees' or 'thugs.' According to Lakshmi Gandhi's NPR news article titled "What a Thug's Life Looked Like in 19th Century India," the historical 'thugs' had a significant impact on British imperialists that left them both fearful and fascinated:

> The word 'thug' traces its roots to the Hindi and Urdu word *thag*, which means thief or swindler, and which itself is derived from the Sanskrit verb sthagati (to conceal). The word would enter the English language in the 1800s during the British imperial rule of India... The thuggees [or thuggee cult] were believed to be a professional organization of criminals and assassins who reportedly had strangled thousands of people on India's roadsides. They were widely portrayed as 'born criminals' who worshipped Kali, the Hindu goddess of death and destruction.

Although the historical 'thuggee cult' was, according to Lakshmi Gandhi, proclaimed to be eradicated by the British, 'the thuggees continued to capture a place in the British imagination even after they were eliminated.' This fascination and fantasization of a thuggee cult extends well beyond 19th century Britain and winds up in American pop culture in a variety of ways. One of the best-known contemporary allusions to the thuggees is in Steven Spielberg's 1984 *Indiana Jones and the Temple of Doom*, where an underground cult sacrifices victims to Kali. Another example is John Ostrander and Luke McDonnell's 1987 comic series *Suicide Squad*. In *Suicide Squad*, one of the main characters, Ravan, is the last living member of a Kali-worshiping thuggee cult.

To better understand our position that Tupac, in his lyrics, reappropriates the story of the real thuggee cult of 19th century India to create his own 'thug life' mythology, we have to understand a little about the goddess Kali to whom the thuggees make their sacrifices, and what we argue Kali means to Tupac. The importance of Kali (or any of her similar 'equivalents' from other traditions) for anyone on the path to enlightenment cannot be understated. More than just the goddess of creative destruction who works in the external world, on the internal path of Hindi enlightenment described in Kundalini Yoga and Tantra (very similar to Vajrayana Buddhism), Kali stands guard over the threshold separating low from high and is considered one of the most challenging barriers a practitioner must cross on their way to awakening. The Kundalini, Tantric path of enlightenment is a passage through the body beginning between the anus and the genitals at the base of the spine. It is there that the 'kunda' or feminine energy is housed. From the base of the spine, the 'kunda serpent' is directed upward through the body before its power culminates in the crown of the head and ultimately passes out into the beyond.

The yogi practitioner uses sacred meditation techniques to direct the fresh earth and water energy of the pelvic floor upward into the heavens of the brain to open the third eye of enlightenment and transcend the separation between ego-self and the godly interconnectivity of the universe. This is why images of Kali depict her standing over the body of Shiva, her male counterpart, holding a man's decapitated head. There are a handful of Kali origin stories. One of our favorites is from *The Linga Purana*. In this text, Shiva, the Hindu god of creative destruction, has to seek the aid of his wife Parvati to slay the demon Daruka because Daruka can be killed only by a female. Parvati becomes a spirit, enters Shiva, mixes with his toxic aspects, reemerges as Kali, and kills Daruka. However, on the battlefield, Kali's lust for blood is so great that she keeps killing and killing until Shiva lies down before her in the form of a child. Kali, also a figure of the divine mother, proceeds to breastfeed the child, who is really Shiva, and Shiva not only sucks breastmilk from Kali but also sucks the anger out of her.

This story makes clear that in the famous image of Kali standing on Shiva's body while holding another man's decapitated head, Shiva and the decapitated man are more or less equivalent, as Shiva's subjugation before Kali is symbolically a form of decapitation or the sacrifice of one's ego. The message is clear – either humble oneself before Kali, as Shiva does, or be humbled by her. All in all, Kail effectively symbolizes one's ongoing process of figuratively shedding one's skin, one's ego, and becoming new. Kali, which means 'the black one,' is associated with darkness because she is the forever-emerging shadow within. In Hinduism, the symbol of decapitation is figurative for a real liberating, internal event or series of events associated with destroying one's propensity toward egocentrism. In Eastern spirituality, the top-down imperialism of the rational mind that imposes its will onto and domesticates the body to pilot it so that it can transform nature into its obedient servant is, contrary to many Western conceptualizations, a sickness that is to be overturned by a bottom-up energy transference. Here, the earth comes first, impressing its knowledge onto the body, and then the body decapitates the ego-head so that the body and the earth are one harmonious flow.

Whether literally involving explicit, sexual yoga practices or metaphorically referencing the process of elevating the kunda energy at the base of the spine up through the body in such a way that it can be conceptualized sexually, these practices are associated with an alternative kind of (inter)course, often an unorthodox type of family, and certainly a different kind of offspring. Whereas the actual 19th-century thuggee cult supposedly made literal sacrifices to Kali, it's easy to consider that a figurative sacrifice to Kali would entail helping give another over to the experience of enlightenment that promises to kill not the literal person but the ego-self preventing one from accessing their full potential. For Tupac, who was no stranger to wordplay, either as code-master using what we've been calling 'reverse doublespeak' or simply as a poet working with figurative language, the word 'Cali,' which is explicitly a shortened version of 'California,' we argue is also implicitly an aural pun referencing the goddess 'Kali.' 'Cali,' for Tupac, as well as 'L.A.' or 'the City of Angels,' were more than literal referents – they were indicators of a way of life and manifestations, both figurative and literal, of the feminine aspect of God. Tupac, in many ways, we argue, worshipped 'Kali,' although he has several names for her, 'Mary' being one many recall him paying homage to, namely in the song 'Hail Mary.'

Mary, like Kali, is a symbolic meditation on how radical presence eradicates the homogeneity of society's filial grasp of the historical timeline and gives birth to newness. This is why, as theologian Dr. John R. Dupuche highlights in his comparative-religion inquiry ("The Goddess Kali and the Virgin Mary") Mary is an abrupt rupture to the Jewish genealogy linking Joseph, Christ's adoptive father, back to Adam, and why, we argue, Christ is considered the last Adam or the end of repetitive time. Because Mary isn't directly connected to the sacred lineage dating back to Eve and then Adam, she is not determined by temporal causality and thus isn't helplessly driven by original sin, a fact that is further highlighted through her Immaculate Conception and her being born without original sin, her being born without Adam's trace. Mary, therefore, like Kali, is effectively beyond history. Where Kali is the female aspect of Shiva that overcomes and decapitates him so that she can give birth to him anew, Mary takes on a similar function in Christianity, albeit connotatively, not denotatively.

The highly implicit riddle of Mary that is hardly ever discussed in orthodox Christian circles is that she is of God or an aspect of God, not unlike how Eve is an aspect of Adam. Following the logic of the traditional 'Genesis' story, Adam is made in God's image and likeness, and Eve is made from an act of dividing Adam or taking a piece of him, which we argue implies two things: (1) Eve was a part of Adam to begin with, or his feminine aspect and (2) if Adam was made in God's image and likeness, and Adam had an original feminine aspect, then God too has a feminine side. Where a unified Adam and Eve are separated in God's creation of Eve, the more traumatizing separation for them isn't the separation itself but their *knowledge* of the separation or their awareness of themselves as binary opposites, which coincides with their expulsion from Eden. Although born of human parents, because she is conceived without original sin, it's implied that Mary is born into existence as a biological phenomenon preceding the physical separation experienced by Adam and Eve. Thus, Mary is more immediately an aspect of God in the way Eve was part of Adam before their division, with the critical difference that when Mary births Christ, opposite Eve coming out of Adam, Mary brings about not a fall from grace but a resuturing between mankind and God. This phenomenon is doubly implied in reverse form when Mary is 'with God's child', or comprises the sacred configuration of a being who houses God directly within her. This image is also easily seen as a dually gendered metaphor for a feminine body with a masculine soul.

The primary meditation that is the riddle of Mary, therefore, invites practitioners to envision her as a kind of forever-transforming radiance of divinity: prior to her birth, Mary is immediately linked with God; then, after her birth, God comes to Mary more or less as a husband comes to his wife, and Mary becomes pregnant with God in the form of Christ. Mary then takes on the role of mother and births her own simultaneous former counterpart and husband as Christ, and then when Christ dies and returns to his Father or God proper, it's as though Christ becomes the Universe again, and Mary now plays the role of the fetus within God in all His vast excellence. It's the image of an infinite flower unfolding into endless fractals. God houses and then births Mary, a pregnant Mary houses and then births God, and then through her Assumption Mary returns to God, and the cycle implicitly repeats with endless immanence and reverberation like a cup forever overflowing. Mary/ Christ is, in summation, a religious symbol for the possibility of a spiritual birth within all humanity that represents humankind's capacity to die and be born again in a manner that transcends a personal and human genealogy.

In 'Hail Mary,' when Tupac invokes Mary, it is this meditation of Mary as the overflowing cup, so similar to the meditation of Kali, that Tupac calls on. The enemies out to get Tupac in 'Hail Mary' are first and foremost enemies that attack him from within, and by evoking Mary as his spirit guide, Tupac is able to do battle with his inner demons:

> Hail Mary catch me if I go
> Let's go deep inside the solitary mind of a madman
> Screams in the dark, evil lurks, enemies, see me flee
> Activate my hate, let it break to the flame
> Set trip, empty out my clip, never stop to aim
> Some say the game is all corrupted
> Fucked in this shit
> Stuck, niggaz is lucky if we bust out this shit
> Plus, mama told me never stop until I bust a nut
> Fuck the world if they can't adjust

It's just as well hail Mary come with me.

In 'Hail Mary,' Tupac takes us 'deep inside the solitary mind of a madman,' where we discover that the real danger here is the absence of motion or the experience of being 'stuck.' This is a particular danger for Tupac and other black youth, but it's also a universal theme that can take on significance for anyone. To oppose this stagnation, Tupac, now referring to Mary as 'mama,' recalls that 'mama told me never stop until I bust a nut,' a phrase that is overlapped with multiple meanings. To 'bust a nut' can refer to a sexual climax, a machine breaking down, and eliminating an insane person or the freedom from insanity. All of the language here is language expressing a kind of desperate groping desire to be free – 'let it break to the flame, empty out my clip never stop to aim' – and Mary, like her Hindu counterpart Kali, is the deity Tupac elicits to aid him in his war against totalitarian fixity.

We get a similar allusion to this unendingly generative intercourse between body and spirit or virgin birth that is constantly welling up from within and shedding layers as it evolves in the more encrypted 'How Do You Want It.' This track, however, in our reading, invokes Kali by name:

> It's like erotic
> Ironic, cause I'm somewhat psychotic
> I'm hitting switches on bitches like I been fixed with hydraulics
> …Nights full of Alize
> A living legend cause you ain't heard about how these niggaz play
> These Cali days.

Tupac, in these lyrics, explicitly positions himself as a 'living legend,' or the mythic body-spirit exchange to which legends refer. Even though, at first listen, it seems as if 'How Do You Want It' is a standard sex song or that it refers to traditional sex, Tupac is quick to dispel these assumptions when he says, 'It's like erotic/ Ironic, cause I'm somewhat psychotic/ I'm hittin switches…' Eroticism, as we know, isn't fornication proper but is more like foreplay, arousal, or nonreproductive intercourse. What the French call *jouissance*. This could, and we argue that it does, mean then that Tupac takes something *similar* to foreplay, arousal, and nonreproductive intercourse (that it's similar and not same is highlighted by Tupac's use of the word 'like' in 'it's like erotic'), and makes a sex song about it, which is, as Tupac confirms, ironic – irony being the opposite of what is expected.

In 'How Do You Want It,' the listener expects the lyrics to denote an exchange between Tupac and another person, if not between Tupac and the listener. However, as Tupac states, the irony is that he's 'somewhat psychotic.' We suggest this means something more along the lines of 'bipolar' or 'schizophrenic' in a divinely figurative sense. 'How Do You Want It,' we argue, is a sex song about generative exchanges between different aspects of Tupac himself that mirror the kinds of unfolding meditations inspired by the imagery of Kali/ Shiva and Mary/ God. This, we argue, is the process of becoming to which Tupac refers when he says, 'I'm hittin switches.' To further corroborate his point in 'How Do You Want It,' just in case the listener doesn't know that this way of life or game is played or practiced day in and day out by adepts, Tupac lets his audience know that this lifestyle does indeed exist and that the name of the game is Kali when he states 'you ain't heard about how these niggaz play…[t]hese Cali days,' which we interpret as, 'You haven't heard about how people play the everyday way of life of Kali, but I'm going to teach you.'

The fact that God in particular and the sacred in general, taking Steinberg at her word, are the subject matter of Tupac's lyrical discourse, without a doubt contributes to the encrypted nature of Tupac's writing. This is especially the case, we argue, because Tupac's conceptualization of God and manner of writing about God comes very close to that of 'apophatic' or 'negative theology,' which, according to philosophy professor Deirde Carabine in an interview titled "Living Without a Why," 'stresses God's absolute transcendence and unknowability in such a way that we cannot say anything about the divine essence because God is so totally beyond being.' If God is beyond being or beyond form and is instead a living, formless becoming, it gets impossible, if not blasphemous, to try and approximate, nail down, or frame God within a single categorical box. Theologians and philosophers, like Plato, whom we know Tupac read, use negative theological reasoning to deploy a poetic language intended to perform the illusiveness of God while simultaneously making God their subject of inquiry.

The most renowned negative theologian in the Jewish tradition is Maimonides, who wrote in the 12th and 13th centuries. In his work on Chabad (an Orthodox Jewish, Hasidic movement that closely studies *The Zohar* and other aspects of *Kabbalah*), titled *Shaar Hayichud Vehaemunah*, Rabbi Yosef Wineberg includes the following quote from Maimonides:

> This [form of unity] wherein G – d's knowledge and so on is one with G – d Himself is beyond the capacity of the mouth to express, beyond the capacity of the ear to hear, and beyond the capacity of the heart of man to apprehend clearly.

Wineberg quotes Maimonides to highlight how human knowledge is distinct from the divine. Maimonides's quote is significant for us not only because it further illuminates negative theology's position that God is almost iconoclastically resistant to representation but also because, when Wineberg quotes Maimonides, he provides an example of how some Jews choose to write the name of God as 'G – d,' which, in the case not only of negative theology but also of Tupac, has radical implications.

It is widespread knowledge that, out of respect for God, some Jews resist writing 'God' and opt for writing 'G – d' instead. This is due to a prohibition in the *Torah* that states that it's unlawful to destroy any text – specifically a Hebrew one – wherein one of the sacredly proper names of God (there are several, 'Yahweh,' meaning 'I am,' being the best known) has been recorded. Because God is eternal, He cannot be destroyed: therefore, erasing God's name is an insult to God and the reality of His everlasting divinity. The seeming irony here is that Jews who write 'G – d' rather than 'God' appear to represent God as an erasure. Although this might seem the opposite of what's intended, it is just another way of expressing the everlasting nature of the Lord because, for these Jews, the quality of God's everlastingness is not fixed but is instead an ongoing process of becoming that is beyond life and death understood as binary opposites. For a Jew practicing negative theology, like Maimonides, this idea gets radicalized to the extent that not only is God's name beyond representation, but everything about God resists fixation because God is synonymous with life or a formation process that exceeds all forms. We suggest that Tupac, a student of Jewish mysticism or *Kabbalah* (which contains its own kind of negative theological reasoning), takes the practice of representing God as an erasure a step further while simultaneously utilizing a political metaphor and encrypting his approach. He does this by signifying God not as 'G – d' but as 'G – .'

For people listening to Tupac who are not subjecting his lyrics to the close analytical scrutiny Steinberg claims they deserve, the abounding instances where Tupac mentions the word 'G' are going to be taken one of two ways, with 'G' either meaning 'gangster' or 'grand' (which is slang for money in general and a thousand dollars specifically). There are significant instances in Tupac, however, where his use of the 'G,' we argue, can also refer to God as an external phenomenon, as an internal potential anyone can access, and as an enlightened teacher dedicated to illuminating the masses. Here, Tupac certainly follows in the footsteps of Hinduism but also, depending on how one interprets a union with God (and God for that matter), also follows logics at play in Buddhism, Gnosticism, Christian mysticism, and *Kabbalah*. To become 'god,' access one's godhood, or awaken the god within is the objective of many spiritual traditions, including the Nation of Islam and the Five-Percent Nation that has dramatically influenced hip-hop culture. All of the 'gods' of those traditions (Buddha, Christ, Allah, Shiva, etc.) thereby function not only as human heroes and prophets who realize their full potential but as models and teachers vowing to lead others to realize the same.

In the Buddhist tradition, after the Buddha (Siddhartha Gautama) reaches enlightenment, he is presented with what seems to be an impasse, an impasse that if better understood will help us understand Tupac's pedagogy. Although the Buddha desires to guide others to learn to move beyond the wheel of death and rebirth, he initially believes enlightenment to be unteachable. However, following a visit from the Hindu gods of old, the Buddha vows to return to the world of suffering, participate in the unending cycle of death and rebirth alongside his fellow human beings, and teach what can be taught of enlightenment. In Buddhism, anyone who seeks enlightenment for the benefit of all sentient beings and thereby follows the Middle Path of the Buddha is called a bodhisattva. In all of its complexity, however, the bodhisattva idea is a problematic concept in Buddhism because it simultaneously refers not only to a practitioner who has already reached enlightenment and has, like the Buddha, vowed to 'joyfully participate in the sorrows of the world' and teach the Middle Path to others but also to someone seeking enlightenment. Dr. Jonathan Silk, professor of Buddhist studies at Leiden University, describes a bodhisattva as follows:

> [E]specially in the Mahayana tradition – the major form of Buddhism in Tibet, China, Korea, and Japan – it was thought that anyone who made the aspiration to awakening (*bodhicittotpada*) – vowing, often in a communal ritual context, to become a Buddha – is therefore a bodhisattva. According to Mahayana teachings, throughout the history of the universe, which had no beginning, many have committed themselves to becoming buddhas. As a result, the universe is filled with a broad range of potential buddhas, from those just setting out on the path of Buddhahood to those who have spent lifetimes in training and have thereby acquired supernatural powers. These 'celestial' bodhisattvas are functionally equivalent to buddhas in their wisdom, compassion, and powers: their compassion motivates them to assist ordinary beings, their wisdom informs them how best to do so, and their accumulated powers enable them to act in miraculous ways.

The above quote highlights the unending praxis of Buddhist practitioners who are simultaneously committed to the ongoing work of their enlightenment and the enlightenment of others, ready, at any given moment, to approach the world as both students and teachers, both as part and as whole. In other words, a true bodhisattva simultaneously seeks enlightenment and is already enlightened.

Bodhisattvas are, in so many words, about the day-to-day business of making 'gods' or 'awakened humans' of both themselves and others. We argue that Tupac, deploying a radical reappropriation of the Jewish practice of omitting letters in the name of God to reference God's excessive vitality and un-representability, both alludes to this bodhisattva vow and names it as his own in many of his songs. 'Death Around the Corner' exemplifies Tupac's bodhisattva vow when Tupac says, 'Got homies in my head that done passed away screamin' please/ Young nigga, make Gs.' In a real Malcolm-X-inspired, black nationalist sense, there is no doubt that both money-making and the business of turning young black men (if not all humans) into 'gangsters' (in the sense that the term means justified soldiers for the betterment and defense of both self and community) were on Tupac's list of things to do. However, given the gravity of the circumstances described in Tupac's lyrics, we argue that 'Gs' in 'Death Around the Corner' also means something like 'gods.'

By all accounts, the idea that the dead would implore the living to make either money or black revolutionaries makes sense. History calls to the living out of a sense of injustice, and no injustice is greater than economic and political injustice. However, the dead also frequently plead with the living out of a sense of moral injustice, begging them to be better people or attain higher spiritual significance. Therefore, the 'Gs' in 'Death Around the Corner' might not only reference money or gangsters. The voices in Tupac's head may implore him from beyond the grave, 'please/ Young nigga make Gs', to say, 'please help our loved ones who are still alive, not only economically and politically, but also, and most importantly, spiritually.' In other words, we argue that, in 'Death Around the Corner,' one of the things the dead are saying is, 'Please save souls.' This point is further corroborated in 'Secretz of War' (off *Still I Rise*), when Tupac says, 'Watch me make' em bleed/ Makin' Gs/ Lord help me with it.' Here, it's clear that the bloody process of making a 'G' is something Tupac evokes God's help in bringing to fruition.

We argue that the 'G' concept is connected to Tupac's notion of what it means to be a 'thug.' Tupac isn't your normal Buddhist bodhisattva. He's takes the Buddhist tradition and twists it into something new. Tupac, to be specific, is a politically active bodhisattva at war with his ego and the egos of others. For Tupac, awakening another isn't only spiritual – it's a potentially viral, political act. By opening another's eyes, Tupac isn't only turning another onto the game or praxis of ego deconstruction – he's making a soldier for a spiritual revolution. This proselytism aspect of Tupac's work is highlighted in 'No More Pain' when Tupac says,

> Mama made me rugged
> Baptized the public
> Now you all thugs, nigga don't you love it.

To be a 'thug' isn't just to be a 'G' or a 'god.' It's to be a frontline warrior struggling for worldwide spiritual awakening. This guru soldier position is abundantly evident in 'Black Jesus' off *Still I Rise*:

> Went to church but don't understand it, they underhanded
> God gave me these commandments, the world is scandalous
> Blast 'til they holy high; baptize they evil minds
> ...In times of war we need somebody raw, rally the troops
> Like a saint that we can trust to help to carry us through
> Black Jesus

We see Tupac stretching here to create a unique synthesis of ideas. A new religion almost or a new spiritual path. He doesn't understand the church, yet he seems more dedicated to God than most. In fact, he's resolved to 'blasting' and 'baptizing' the 'evil minds' that populate the world of suffering. The deity Tupac evokes in this dedication – Black Jesus – isn't God. He's a saint who will carry people not only through the challenging, dangerous process of enlightenment but through the work of 'saving others,' the work of the bodhisattva. 'Rally the troops,' he says. This isn't just theology for Tupac. It's warfare.

Tupac's 'thug life,' bodhisattva vow is a war of words that reorients and integrates two separate yet overlapping worlds – the realm of enlightenment (a spiritual world with its own codes and sign systems), and the 'ordinary' world and culture one dwelled in prior to enlightenment, which, in Tupac's case, is a world of 'drug dealers, thugs, and killers.' Both the internal and external aspects of Tupac's war against egomania are underscored perfectly in 'No More Pain,' when Tupac says,

> My only fear of death is reincarnation
> Heart of a soldier with the brain to teach a whole nation
> And feelin no more pain.

Like the overflowing cup that is Kali and Mary, Tupac's war is directed at destroying homogeneity within and without. His only fear of death is 'reincarnation' or repetition, both socially and personally. Moreover, we believe Tupac wished that there would never have to be another 'him' in the sense that he hoped that he would die having completed his job, thus making it unnecessary for another to carry on his work in the same manner he did. So, in this way, he also wishes never to repeat, to never be reincarnated.

The imperative to attain nirvana by preventing rebirth is the central theme of the brilliant *Tibetan Book of the Dead*, which we know Tupac read, a book that in Tibetan culture isn't only a literal guide for the dying as they transition between lives but is also a guide for the living. Like the dead, the living are stuck in the cycle of death and rebirth. They are always about the business of dying and transitioning between 'lives' or different phases of life. Their cells regenerate and they ejaculate and menstruate and defecate and cut their hair and fingernails, and their cup continues to overflow in the myriad of ways it always does – death, rebirth, over and over. To live the code of a 'G' and practice the art of 'thug life,' for Tupac, is, in its external aspect, a pedagogical war waged against egocentrism and rebirth or repetition. Tupac stresses this in 'No More Pain' by saying he has 'the heart of a soldier with the brain to teach a whole nation with no more pain.' Here, it isn't only that Tupac is arguing that he is, in a sense, beyond pain. He's also highlighting his paradoxical imperative to help deliver a similar state to others, not by taking them away from pain but helping guide them through it. This is clear in the chorus of 'No More Pain' when Tupac states, 'I came to bring the pain/ Hardcore to the brain' before inviting listeners to face their pain by turning inward when he says, 'Let's go inside my astral plane' or one's inner dimension to come face to face with oneself.

Two critical aspects of the bodhisattva must be underscored again to appreciate how Tupac capitalizes on that rich tradition in his lyrics. A bodhisattva, firstly, doesn't awaken their god nature by avoiding pain but by turning within and soldiering through. Secondly, after reaching enlightenment (if we can pretend for a moment that it's just one event and not an ongoing process), the bodhisattva returns to their community, not as an alien god with all the answers who lectures to 'idiots' about a better way of life and expects to be followed. As the bodhisattva turns within himself and confronts suffering inside to move through and, in some ways, beyond it, so the bodhisattva returns to his former community and works from within it alongside his fellow community members to teach through example. We understand this to be what Niccolò Machiavelli, the 16th century Italian philosopher Tupac renamed himself after (Makaveli) on his fifth studio album, refers to in different words in *The Prince* when he says, 'And above all things, a prince ought to live amongst his people in such a way that no unexpected circumstances, whether of good or evil, shall make him change.' We can hear Tupac echoing this sentiment in 'Until the End of Time:'

> When my mama ask me will I change
> I tell her yeah but it's clear I'll always be the same
> Until the end of time.

When change is all that is consistent, the work of everyday life becomes the work of discerning the most advantageous way to go about changing.

More familiar to students of Western spirituality, this art of esoterically working within a system to alter it is what St. Paul alludes to in his luminous statement from *First Corinthians*, 9:20-22:

> And unto the Jews I became as a Jew, that I might gain the Jews; to them that are under the law, as under the law, that I might gain them that are under the law; to them that are without law, as without law, (being not without law to God, but under the law to Christ,) that I might gain them that are without law. To the weak became I as weak, that I might gain the weak: I am made all things to all men, that I might by all means save some.

Here, we argue, it's not just that St. Paul speaks on behalf of his cryptic pedagogy that can adapt to any environment but that, in his 'being all things to all men that he might save some,' St. Paul personifies a living, breathing, and evolving God that can emerge from within anyone, anywhere, and yet cannot, due to his excessive un-representability, be known in advance. Like St. Paul, we argue, Tupac speaks poetry with mindfulness to God to open up a doorway of possibility for God to enter as He pleases.

Speaking to some combination of meditation practice and writing process, in 'Ghetto Gospel,' Tupac says,

> If I upset you, don't stress
> Never forget that God isn't finished with me yet
> I feel his hand on my brain
> When I write rhymes I go blind and let the Lord do his thing.

With 'Ghetto Gospel,' we advance our understanding of Tupac's esotericism even more. Not only is he speaking a code for spiritual revolutionaries, as Steinberg suggests, and using a kind of reverse doublespeak intended to knock out enemies both without and within, like we get from Dyson, Tupac also spits the raw, poetic language of the unconscious so that we the listeners can hear that language more clearly within ourselves and thereby come to know ourselves not as individuals but as the whole network of living interconnectivity that we are.

In 4:10-12 from *The Gospel of Mark,* when his disciples ask him why he speaks in parables, Jesus esoterically responds with the following parable:

> Because it is given unto you to know the mysteries of the kingdom of heaven, but to them it is not given. For whosoever hath, to him shall be given, and he shall have more abundance: but whosoever hath not, from him shall be taken away even that he hath. Therefore speak I to them in parables: because they seeing see not; and hearing they hear not, neither do they understand.

Those who approach Christ's words from within – where they not only already have unspeakable biological wealth but where the language of the unconscious, myths, dreams, and poetry already lives – will, when hearing Jesus' parable, be able to capitalize on His words and further advance their knowledge of themselves in an immense sense. By finding Christ inside themselves, they can grow themselves through Christ. But those who approach Christ and His words as though He and what He says come only from another place without will hear only inconsistent paradoxes. We suggest that the same applies to Tupac and that it's within the living tradition out of which divine figures like Jesus speak and act that Tupac sees and situates himself.

Buddha Statue, near Belum Caves, Andhra Pradesh, India

Kali.

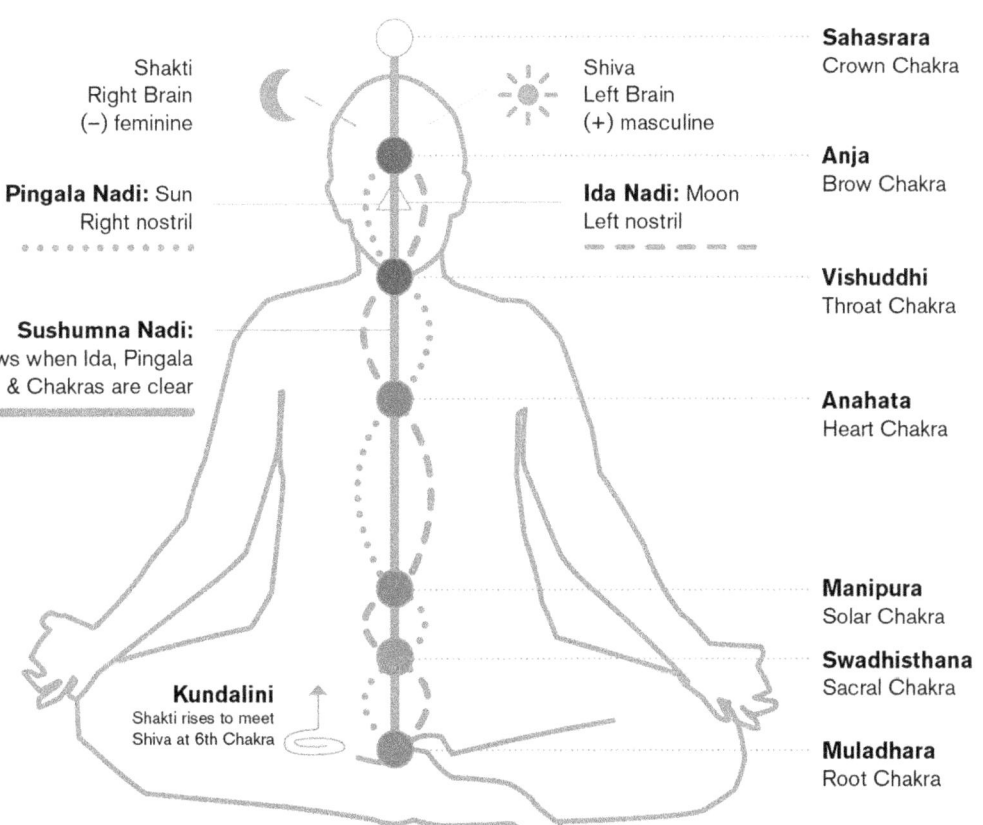

Diagram of chakras and kundalini.

Chapter 1

Tupac's Skand(h)as

> 'The unconscious disguising of physiological requirements under the cloak of the objective, the ideal, the purely spiritual, is carried on to an alarming extent, and I have often enough asked myself, whether on the whole philosophy hitherto has not generally been merely an interpretation of the body, and a misunderstanding of the body.'
>
> Friedrich Nietzsche from the preface to the second edition of *The Joyful Wisdom.*

Tupac's track 'Skandalouz,' from his fourth studio album, *All Eyez On Me,* is where we must begin our closer inquiry into the highly political spirituality of Shakur because it best summarizes the internal threat against which Tupac directs his always-evolving sacred practice. From the level of a surface reading, 'Skandalouz' is not only a song about a specifically scandalous girl the speaker meets and has intercourse with before she double-crosses him by publicly pretending the two have never met. It also refers to a type of girl in general who is described as not only 'phony' and 'back-stabbing' but also as thieving: 'This bitch'll have ya wakin up with all your cash missin.' There is an element of ironic revenge in the song, as it ends with the speaker embodying the traits of the scandalous girl and getting over on her (or one of her kind) before she can take advantage of him:

> Before I let her get me, I got her
> Went in her purse and took a hundred dollars
> Cause nigga I'm so scandalous.

This ironic twist at the end, which blurs the boundary separating the speaker from the girl he describes, causes the reader to loop back to the beginning of the song and re-experience it with complete uncertainty as to whether the two can ever be separated in the first place.

As we elaborated in the introduction, Tupac was well versed in psychology, philosophy, and especially sacred texts, many that to a traditional religious practitioner in the West would seem esoteric. For a reader to experience the full depth of 'Skandalouz,' some spiritual background knowledge is necessary, specifically some knowledge of Hinduism and Buddhism, two traditions from which we know Tupac drew inspiration. From our position, Tupac deliberately spells the word 'scandalous' as 'skandalouz' to allude to Hinduism and Buddhism. The word 'skanda' is a Sanskrit translation, and it can refer to separate deities in both Hinduism and Buddhism. In addition, 'skanda' is only one letter away from being 'skandha,' a foundational Buddhist concept. More still, along these homophonous lines, whenever the word 'skanda' is spoken, 'skandha' (spelled with an 'h') can also be heard and vice versa. Therefore, we suggest that, with Tupac, not only are the different meanings of the word 'skanda' connected in both Hinduism and Buddhism but they are also connected to the Buddhist concept of the 'skandhas.'

New religions emerge from old religions. Christianity from Judaism. Buddhism from Hinduism. In Western orthodox Christian and Jewish circles, however, where there are often rigid distinctions separating the Old Testament and Judaism from the New Testament and Christianity, we argue that this is less the case between Hinduism and Buddhism. This isn't to say that there aren't certain Buddhists and Hindus who make clear distinctions between themselves or that there aren't technical details the two groups disagree on because there are. Regardless, Hindus and Buddhists recognize that their traditions are connected in a more fluid way than the more rigid connection, first linking and then firmly separating Jews, Christians, and even Muslims. Hindus and Buddhists emphasize that enlightenment can happen in many ways and on varying levels. So, for most Hindus and Buddhists, whatever truth or text leads one to a more profound understanding is the right one. With Jews, Christians, and Muslims, however, there is frequently the sense that their sacred texts, respectively, are superior. All of this is to say that when Tupac lays out a shifting continuum between Hindu and Buddhist terms, he is in no way working outside the traditions of Hinduism and Buddhism.

In Hinduism, Brahman is the ultimate, universal reality. Brahman is the Hindus' most awesome, large-scale concept of God. Brahman is the Holy Spirit-like, universal ether that lives in, vitalizes, and evolves throughout all of existence. Atman, in contrast, is the small-scale Hindu concept of the soul. The Atman is a microcosmic, internal manifestation of Brahman. For many Hindus, the goal of the yogic path is to use meditation techniques to awaken oneself to the vital reality that their Atman is Brahman. The goal, in other words, is to realize that God and self are one. Tupac, as mentioned in the introduction, sees this goal as the business of making 'Gs' or making 'gods.' Helping people awaken their God consciousness. Helping people experience their Atman as Brahman. The vast numbers of Hindu deities are, likewise, also manifestations of the multidimensional characteristics and functionalities of Brahman. So, for Hindus, Skanda (also known as Kartikeya) is the god of sacred war, not wholly dissimilar from Kali, the goddess of creation and destruction we mentioned in the introduction. They are similar insofar as Skanda, like Kali, is ultimately an avatar of Brahman or another door to Brahman. Understanding Skanda, however, comes with nuances that further open our understanding of Hinduism and Tupac's revolutionary, sacred politics.

The word 'Skanda' comes from 'skandr,' meaning to 'spill, ooze, leap, attack.' According to *The Illustrated Encyclopedia of Hinduism: N-Z* by professor of religion and Asian studies Dr. James Lochtefeld, Skanda comes into being because 'Shiva and Parvati are disturbed while making love, and Shiva inadvertently spills his semen on the ground.' Shiva (the destroyer) is one of the principal deities in Hinduism, along with Vishnu (the preserver) and Brahma (the creator). Parvati is the wife of Shiva, distinct from Kali, who is Shiva's consort. Skanda is the product of Shiva's spilled semen running from the ground and taking root in the River Ganges, which is then heated by the god Agni. Depicted as decked in weapons, riding a peacock, and sometimes having six heads (representative of the six mothers who raised him following his birth), Skanda is the philosopher-warrior god of Hinduism. Following his birth, Skanda – child of earth, water, sun, and deity – defeats the demon Taraka before teaching all living beings enlightenment.

In Buddhism, similar to Hinduism, the word 'Skanda' refers to a famous bodhisattva who is the guardian of sacred teachings. Like the Skanda of Hinduism, the Buddhist bodhisattva is depicted clad with weaponry, and the similarities between these sacred warriors and Tupac (whose name alone means 'intelligent warrior') should not be lost on readers. The 'skandhas' (with an 'h') in Buddhism, however, are a foundational component of its unique account of inner spirituality. Buddhists don't have a word for an eternal soul that exists before a body, lives in a body, and leaves the body to return to some other plane of existence, as is the case with Christianity, Judaism, and Islam. Nor do Buddhists exactly believe in a soul that dies and is born again as another lifeform, as is the manner of thought proper to Hinduism. The German philosopher Friedrich Nietzsche (whom we know Tupac also read) expresses a sentiment on the nonexistence of the soul similar to that of the Buddhists. In *Thus Spake Zarathustra*, Nietzsche says, 'Body am I entirely, and nothing more; and soul is only the name of something about the body.' By describing the soul as 'something *about* [our italics] the body,' Nietzsche is marking that which is mistakenly categorized as soul as the material both *of the body* and *that which passes through it*, 'about' being synonymous with 'concerning' or having to do with, which, when applied to the body, refers to all that is in proximity to it both inside and out.

The concept of the 'skandhas' in Buddhism comes close to Nietzsche's account of that which others mistake as the 'soul.' 'Skandha' means 'heaps, aggregates, collections, groupings.' There are five 'aggregates' or skandhas in Buddhism, and together they comprise the totality of the human body's mental and physical makeup. The five aggregates are form, sensations, perceptions, mental activity, and consciousness. For Buddhists, when a person is born, they go from place to place, and, when they do, their body absorbs that environment. They eat, are aroused, see and hear, produce neurotransmitters, and so forth. Their body then holds onto those 'aggregates,' or that 'heap,' for however long their shelf lives last or its shelf life lasts. Then the aggregates are excreted and menstruated and ejaculated and sweated out or whatever the case may be, and thereby the subject's mentality and sense of identity also changes. All inner aggregates are connected to and disconnected from one another, but Buddhism has no coherent sense of soul or even identity. There are no individual beings, only evolving becomings, because as any part or skandha changes, the whole being changes (from outside in to inside out). In this chapter, because every singular implies a plural and vice versa, we sometimes use the word 'skandha' to refer to the whole heap or assemblage of the five skandhas and each of the individual skandhas.

It is the *materiality* of the philosopher war god Skanda from Hinduism (the 'ooze' born of semen, earth, water, sunlight, and deity) that so clearly connects the god to the Buddhist concept of the five skandhas of aggregates. But the connection between the Skanda of Buddhism and the skandhas of Buddhism, however, is a more difficult one to make. However, we can begin to lay a foundation for this link by making known that, for Buddhists, their primary concern regarding the skandhas is that if one possessively clings to a particular 'heap' for too long, it will bring about a great many negative results. It will, in Tupac's terms, result in their being trapped, 'You know they got me trapped in this prison of seclusion/ Happiness, living on the streets is a delusion.' What gives Tupac's lyrics an added kick that Buddhism frequently lacks, however, is that in the song 'Trapped,' off *2Pacalypse Now*, Tupac complicates the business of oneself clinging to delusions by adding in the element of social control and ideology. It's unclear in Tupac whether the desire to cling to fixity is some flaw of the mind, some manner of social conditioning, or both.

In *You Are Here: Discovering the Magic of the Present Moment*, Vietnamese Buddhist Thich Nhat Hanh describes the potential problem with the skandhas:

> There is no such thing as a self, no absolute, permanent entity to be found in the element we call 'body.' In our ignorance, we believe there is a permanent entity in us, and our pain and suffering manifest based on that ignorance.

Cognitive dissonance occurs if one identifies with or clings to any aggregate for too long. Not only between oneself and the world but also within oneself. Addressing the same problem differently, tongue in cheek, in *Thus Spake Zarathustra*, Nietzsche says, 'A light has dawned upon me: I need companions – living ones; not dead companions and corpses, which I carry with me wherever I go.' Here, Zarathustra, the protagonist of Nietzsche's philosophic narrative and no doubt a foil for Nietzsche himself, uses the word 'companions' to refer both to his inside or 'skandhas' and to any student who would study under him, stating not only that he seeks students who aren't so attached to themselves that they are effectively 'corpses', but also that he seeks a life-affirming relationship with himself, not one where he drags around a 'corpse' of attachment.

One fundamental connection bridging the warlike and guardian aspect of both the Skanda of Hinduism and the Skanda of Buddhism to the Buddhist skandhas is, we argue, the potentially inimical nature of the skandhas thus described. Here, however, the matter becomes complicated. On the one hand, we can say that it is a 'corpse skandha' or a skandha one can't release that both the philosopher warrior of Hinduism does battle against and the guardian bodhisattva of Buddhism keeps watch for. On the other hand, however, due to an over-attached or repressed skandha's tendency to present itself as an inner-war-god in the form of an ego dictator, we *could* easily misinterpret the symbolism of the war deity of Hinduism and the guardian bodhisattva of Buddhism and perceive them not as the aids one calls on to overthrow a clung skandha but rather as the attached 'corpse skandha' itself in a deceptive form.

To help clarify and qualify the problem that Buddhists conceptualize as a skandha made precarious through overattachment, we segue to psychoanalysis founder Sigmund Freud's notion of the ego ideal established in his groundbreaking essay "On Narcissism." Moreover, because Freud's "On Narcissism" places particular emphasis on sexual repression as it relates to something similar to the Buddhist notion of an over-attached skandha, turning to Freud will help gear us up to approach the problem as Tupac wrestles with it in 'Skandalouz,' because 'Skandalouz' is organized as a song about a sexual relationship. Freud's often-cited weakness, however, is that he overemphasizes sexual repression opposite the more comprehensive Buddhist approach to attachment, making it so that we can imagine Freud, as an analyst and literary critic, would never be able to consider the possibility that sexual repression in Tupac's song functions as a metaphor for repression on a grander scale. More importantly, nor would he be able to see how Tupac reappropriates the ongoing theme in mysticism as a genre that figures sex as a metaphor for all things generative, and how Tupac particularizes it to himself, his community, and his time.

In "On Narcissism," Freud's term 'narcissism' is a technical term that operates very differently than how the word is commonly used. 'Narcissism' isn't only a complex or an abnormality some individuals suffer from. Narcissism is a mental and physical functionality at work in all humans at varying degrees of intensity. Narcissism, for Freud, accounts for not only what happens when one overtly treats their own body like the body of one they sexually desire; it also points to 'part of the normal functioning of libido' related to autoeroticism. Autoeroticism isn't just masturbation for Freud. It's commonplace arousal that occurs during dreams, daydreams, encounters with people who excite oneself, and other random incidents of stimulation involving the erogenous zones. Freud claims that autoeroticism happens frequently and that the libidinal energy generated by autoerotic narcissism, or arousal that doesn't lead to sexual climax, ultimately accumulates in the body and, domino-effect-like, back-presses on the whole organism until it culminates to construct in the mind a shifting and complicated ideal version both of others and of oneself that he calls the 'ego ideal.'

Freud describes the 'ego ideal' that is produced as the mental corollary of narcissistic, libidinal repression:

> This ego ideal is now the target of the self-love which was enjoyed in childhood by the actual ego… What he projects before him as his ideal is the substitute for the lost narcissism of his childhood in which he was his own ideal.

So every time one has a dream, daydream, a real encounter with another person, or a random stimulation, the libidinal energy the body biologically prepares for another gets redirected. This repressed libidinal energy builds a fake other or ideal within that gets projected onto and outside of oneself, as the ideal can present as both an ideal version of oneself and another. For Freud, this fake ideal is a psychic substitute for the experience of narcissistic wholeness that one perceived oneself to be wrapped within during that phase of childhood where one couldn't distinguish oneself from their mother or anyone or anything else.

So, according to Freud in "On Narcissism," even when one is engaged in a relationship with another person, they are also generating and having an affair with this other within that gets recorded and projected without as an ideal, which would explain why in 'All About U' – note the letter 'U' whose shape suggests something like a boomerang effect – Tupac sees 'the same ho' everywhere he goes. 'Every other city we go, every other video (It's all about you)/ No matter where I go, I see the same ho.' This track, off *All Eyez On Me*, is certainly about 'groupies,' as the song makes clear, but we're thinking 'groupies' might also have other significance. Groupies may signify the skandhas – which are also called the groupings or aggregates – and the kinds of symptomatic mental images and sounds they manifest. For Freud, at the same time one is engaged in this inner relationship with this ideal that one projects outside of oneself onto the world, one, in their exchanges with others, is also continuously engaged in this war within themselves where they slip in and out of the ideal they strive to achieve and present to others. Moreover, the ego ideal in Freud also functions as an internal police officer who watches, judges, and enforces the so-called normality of the social order. Freud says,

> In addition to its individual side, this ideal has a social side; it is also the common ideal of a family, a class or a nation.

Freud is saying here that redirected sexual energy is not natural but is socially imposed. Because it is imposed from the outside, at some point, the work of resisting one's nature on behalf of the social forces restricting it (state and family) get internalized so that they operate independently of external pressures. Therefore, the internal repressive mechanism – the ego ideal – can take on the characteristics of the people most active in permitting libidinal energy from following its natural course. This is how the ego ideal develops an internal voice that can switch between sounding like mom and dad, teacher, boss, and political leader. It is very much an inner policing apparatus, and, although we in no way deny that Tupac was very much at war with the literal police, we also suggest that he was additionally at war with this internal policing mechanism. Moreover, we suggest that Tupac understood the connection between the two, the police without and the police within. In Freud, the ego ideal is the agent of conformity, a disciplinary model for both self and other, and, just like a skandha to which one excessively clings, the repressive core of the ego ideal has the potential to bring about serious physical ailments and mental health disorders.

Because there is an aspect of a repressed skandha that is decidedly sexual and markedly autoerotic, as Freud makes clear in his analysis of the ego ideal, we have no doubt that the skandhas tend to be evident to those determined to master or understand the sexual arts. And this theme of sex power is pervasive not only in Tupac but in all of hip-hop. With the specific case of Tupac, however, those who know Tupac's biography can infer this will to sex power into the gap separating the young Tupac who studied dance and theater, as well as the early teen Tupac who danced (sometimes in leopardskin Speedo's) with the Digital Underground, from the older Tupac, who was the representative of 'thug life.' Power. Money. Sexual prowess. Also along these lines, because of its sexual dimension, we suspect (as does Jung, whom we will analyze further momentarily) that the psychic echo of a repressed skandha (the ego ideal) is frequently gendered as feminine by men presenting as heterosexual. In other words, regarding the latter point, when a man who identifies as heterosexual has a conscious sexual fantasy, either when masturbating or having intercourse with a woman, he also fantasizes about a series of women, a single woman, or a composite woman made up of many women. But despite the man's fantasy, he is, first and foremost, working only with his own body and his own male biological capacity to imagine. This is the case until the man fully confronts himself and accepts the sexual dimension of 'skandha.' By accepting the sexual functionality of skandha, the man begins to see 'her' not in 'her' dimension as a fantasy *product* but as the foundation for and raw material of fantasy *production*.

❖

This is why, in Tupac's 'Skandalouz,' what the speaker says of the 'girl' we argue can operate as a metaphor for the skandhas: 'She got a body make a mother fucker fantasize.' Even after a man openly identifying as heterosexual begins to reconceptualize skandha as something more like network chakra energy flows, or what is sometimes called the subtle body, and not as a fantasy lover, as we argue is the case with Tupac, he might continue to conceptualize the skandha and represent the skandha as feminine, either for those who haven't advanced in their understanding of themselves or as a code for those who have. In our minds, a clear instance of Tupac conceptualizing the liberated skandhas or the liberated subtle body not as a veiled feminine other but as a chakra network can be seen in the song 'Thugz Mansion,' off the album *Better Dayz*, where, similar to Christian mystic St. Teresa of Avila's *Interior Castle*, Tupac's 'soul' is depicted as a vast and complex palace full of the spirits of his ancestors.

Now that we've defined the Skandas of Hinduism and Buddhism, the Buddhist concept of the skandhas, and Freud's notion of narcissistic autoeroticism, as well as established a general parameter within which they intersect, we turn our attention to Freud's once student and then opponent, Swiss psychiatrist and psychoanalyst Carl Gustav Jung for the final component of our analytical framework. Jung is imperative to our analysis for two reasons: the way he accounts for the human tendency to gender the ego ideal (itself the echo of a repressed skandha) and his simplified (and popularized) teleology of enlightenment called 'the individuation process.' According to Jung, humans have 'a natural religious function' that Jung terms 'the individuation process.' We propose that Jung's 'individuation process' will help clarify how Tupac develops the plot in 'Skandalouz,' which maps the speaker's progression from being terrorized by the feminized skand(h)a to embodying 'her' power. The speaker in 'Skandalouz' ascends through levels of understanding, as does a person undergoing Jung's 'individuation process,' which is also why we suggest that the 'individuation process' (or any other name for the levels of enlightenment) is frequently one of the things Tupac alludes to when he mentions 'the game.' In the introduction, we mentioned how Tupac, like Ram Dass, alludes to the game as the art of living in the world while also not becoming too attached to it, while, in other words, also recognizing its illusory aspects. To be clear, this aspect of playing the game isn't disconnected from Jung's individuation process or the idea of enlightenment as levels of advancement one must move through as though playing a video game, because the individuation process is just as much about moving through stages of illusion as it is about advancing through stages of knowledge.

Jung's individuation process is the procedure whereby one integrates their collective unconscious into the everyday world of their ego consciousness to achieve a 'wholeness' that does not make them 'complete' in a closed loop of fixed finality, nor does it make them an 'individual' with an unchangeable essence. It makes them *individuated* – a specific singularity or network of multiple, interlinking intelligences connecting consciousness, the unconscious, society, and one's surrounding environment. From our understanding, an individuated person is similar to the Overman Nietzsche describes in *Thus Spake Zarathustra*. An individuated person is enlightened, in other words. They don't strive to leave the body and the earth and fly off into some other heavenly world. They surpass the isolated category of humanity by not only climbing up but also by descending down the figurative sacred mountain, climbing down out of the heavens into the world of plants and animals to fashion themselves anew.

For those inspired by Jung, like psychologist John Rowan, there are more or less distinct stages in the individuation process:

> There is often a movement from dealing with persona at the start... to the ego at the second stage, to the shadow at the third stage, to the anima or animus, [and] to the Self at the final stage.

Unpacking the stages of Jung's individuation process requires briefly defining basic Jungian terminology. For Jung, one both consciously and unconsciously creates a persona. The persona is like that aspect of Freud's ego ideal that gets projected both onto oneself and outward onto the world. It's both the mask one wears to present oneself in public and the standard against which one measures others' normalcy. In his 1995 interview at Clinton Correctional Facility, Tupac clarifies that he is not a persona and that he is at war with rappers who present themselves falsely:

> If we do wanna live the thug life and the gangster life and all that, okay, stop being cowards, and let's have a revolution, but we don't wanna do that. Dudes just wanna live a character. They wanna be cartoons…

For Jung, simultaneously and as a corollary to the persona, one generates both an antithesis shadow-self and an animus or anima. The shadow is a living counterpart to and a by-product of the persona. However, because it's the aspect of the self that the conscious mind can't accept, one represses and imprisons it within the depths of one's interior. The animus and anima are one's own inner gender negatives. As Tupac says in 'Fake Ass Bitches,' off *R U Still Down (Remember Me),* 'Most of these niggas be bitches too/ But you'll never hear that side of the story.' The animus and anima too are repressed shadow-selves, but they are specifically repressions that have gendered qualities. Jung refers to the subjective interior of repression as the personal unconscious juxtaposed to the collective unconscious. For Jung, the personal unconscious is the storehouse of personally repressed history, but the collective unconscious is the concealed database that contains the history of humanity's ongoing and constantly updating evolutionary development. It's both the evolutionary history and the evolutionary potential shared in common between members of the human race. Between the personal and the collective unconsciousness is the ego. The ego is the conscious mediator between not just the personal and collective unconscious but between all psychic worlds. It is the place from which one speaks when one says 'I,' 'me,' or 'mine.'

Jung claims that every man conceals within him a portion of his 'spirit' that he unconsciously conceptualizes as 'feminine,' and he calls this the anima. Women, antithetically, keep veiled within themselves a portion of their 'spirit' that they unconsciously assign 'masculine' attributes to, and Jung terms this the animus. From our perspective, Jung's account of the anima/ animus comes very close to the sexual and gendered aspects associated with skandha we've already analyzed in Freud. As mentioned, Jung's anima/ animus is basically a gendered manifestation of Freud's ego ideal, and the ego ideal in Freud (similar to Buddhism) has a material, biological base. It comes from repressed libidinal energy. We suggest that Buddhists refer to a similar base but just reference it as a repressed or blocked skandha, a repressed or blocked skandha that manifests a wrathful dakini (their language for addressing what Jung would call an anima in its angry permutation). In Jung, the anima/ animus are the repressed materials that the psyche subconsciously genders as they pass through the body, are generated by the body, and lodge inside the body, as well as the body's repressed or ignored anatomical regions.

Jung goes further than Freud by tracking how the repressed skandha and the repressed ego ideal it generates can become known and thereby transformed through the individuation process. In Jung, awareness of the anima/ animus marks a different understanding of the shadow-self, signaling progression beyond the personal unconscious toward the collective unconscious. But we argue that one doesn't necessarily perceive their anima/ animus as positive indicators signaling spiritual advancement. We argue that there can be shadow or personal unconscious versions of the animus (her wrathful form) and that Tupac presents us with such a version with vivid imagery and poetic dexterity in 'Skandalouz.' Regarding the shadow-anima, the feminine shadow engendered by a repressive male persona, Jung states:

> Identity with the persona automatically leads to an unconscious identity with the anima (for men) because, when the ego is not differentiated from the persona, it can have no conscious relation to the unconscious process... Moreover, the anima is inevitably projected upon a real object [object here simultaneously refers to another person without and a repressed skandha within], with which he gets into a relation of almost total dependence.

Until the ego can cease identifying with the persona and integrate the living, collective-unconscious anima into its conscious existence, the shadow-anima appears only as a fake by-product or mirror opposite of the falsity that is the persona (the 'Bonnie Parker' to the 'Clyde Barrow' one strives to be, to use a Tupac-esque gangster-inspired analogy). So long as this stage prevails, according to Jung, the persona-man is addictively dependent on women to validate his self-worth, so the persona-man constantly strives to domesticate and control women.

Persona-man is constantly falling in love with the personal unconscious in the form of shadow-anima – in a word, he's constantly falling in love with his own externally-projected feminized ideal, comprising both memories and fantasies. At the same time persona-man is perpetually falling in and out of love with the shadow-anima, he is also both resisting and falling in love with the collective-unconscious-anima or personified and feminized life itself. The fully liberated skandhas. The activated subtle body. Because persona-man cannot fully recognize his love of life this way, he deceives himself into creating an illusory dependency on an individual woman or series of predictable women he psychically mistakes as life in feminine form. To sustain his illusory masculinity, persona-man needs an antithetical and equally fake gender opposite to shore up his fantasy. In other words, if he's going to tell the story to himself and others that he's 'Clyde Barrow,' he needs a 'Bonnie Parker.' Because persona-man, at this stage, is unable to reconcile with himself the truth that his love of the freedom he sees in another is in reality a love of the potential freedom he both conceals within himself and doesn't access in the world, he seeks to control himself by controlling his lover(s) and ultimately fails on both fronts. Tupac has more songs about how men should resist being dependent on and controlled by women to list. 'Wonder Why They Call U,' off *All Eyez On Me*, however, stands out because it's a track about a woman who turns herself into an object in the hope of gaining control over men, only to have her plan backfire on her. Rather than controlling men, the woman (or type of woman) in the song winds up being controlled by them. Then, additionally, 'I Get Around,' off *Strictly 4 My N.I.G.G.A.Z*, comes to mind when Tupac sarcastically says,

> All respect to those who break their neck to keep their hoes in check

> Cause hoes they sweat a brother majorly
> And I don't know why your girl keeps paging me

Very much playing the Dozens here, Tupac is being ironic. It's useless for anyone to break their neck to police the person they are in a relationship with because that person will always lust after someone else. Whether they cheat physically, mentally, or emotionally does matter, but the idea that one's romantic partner will undyingly desire them and only them is a complete fantasy. Tupac knows this, and, true to the real spirit of the Dozens, he can't level his critique against another without also accepting its truth himself.

To break away from this conscious identification with the persona and unconscious identification with the shadow-anima that leads to an unhealthy dependence on women, Jung states that one ultimately must undergo the final stage of the individuation process and 'become woman:'

> The most masculine man needs women, and he is consequently their slave. Become a woman yourself, and you will be saved from slavery to women… [T]hrough becoming a woman you attain freedom from women and their tyranny. The acceptance of femininity leads to completion.

The Self is the highest achievement of Jung's individuation process, and the Self is simply (for men) the anima no longer conceived of as a concealed, internalized other within but as a once-alienated and now fully-integrated aspect of oneself. The Whole Self in Jung is sometimes figured as a wise old man; a man, like Christ, who is not a persona of masculinity but is instead a man who, in fully accepting his wisdom, compassion, and femininity, is beyond gender. However, regarding Jung's individuation process, what may at first appear to follow a series of teleological stages or what might easily be intellectually presented as a progressive chronology, is quite possibly a much more complex and disorganized process of unending cycles and practices of growth that take one through an infinite plethora of self-to-skandha configurations.

To clarify, we understand the Buddhist concept of skandha as a catch-all for both Jung's personal and collective unconscious: personal when skandha is more or less repressed and collective when it's more or less liberated. Skandhas are aggregates of the outside world concealed and congealed within. The more those aggregates are repressed and the more they are personalized the more they work to create myopic individuals. The more one becomes aware of their skandhas, however, the more those skandhas are not only allowed to flow freely inside and outside of the body, but the more one can perceive the skandhas and themselves as belonging to an infinitely deep, geologic timeline. This is how we understand individuation for Jung.

Now that we have basic background knowledge regarding the skandas of both Hinduism and Buddhism, the Buddhist skandhas, Freud's concept of narcissism, the unique role the anima plays in Jung's individuation process, and the crossroads where all these ideas converge, we can dive below the depths of surface analysis into the complex genius of Tupac's track 'Skandalouz' by interpreting the 'girl' in the song as a figure for the skand(h)as. Explaining how Tupac sets up the 'girl' in 'Skandalouz' to be a figure for the skand(h)as (both repressed and unrepressed) first requires us to closely tune our ears into not only Tupac's lyrics but how his lyrics parallel and work with the background sounds established by producer Daz Dillinger on the track. The extent to which Dillinger and vocalist Nate Dogg were in on Tupac's working Hindu-Buddhist concepts into the song or were guided by Tupac in their work on the track remains unknown. However, the sounds on the song must be analyzed to fully capture what Tupac is up to. Tupac's opening line on 'Skandalouz' is 'I met ya through my homie now ya act like ya don't know me,' but right as he delivers his first line, Dillinger layers into the background what sounds like flushing water overlapped with an outflow of breath. The effect, when analyzed alongside Tupac's lyrics, produces in the listener the image of something spirit-like entering the body as though the breath of life were flushed or breathed into it, so that when Tupac says, 'I met you through my homie,' it's as though the 'you' refers to the flushing-breath sound (skandha in its anima form) and 'homie' signifies the speaker's body.

Regarding these lyrics and the sound, it's as though at the beginning of the track Tupac presents us with a very Western, Cartesian depiction of the body. There's mind, body, and soul. The mind is the place where the speaker of the track lives. It's the space from which the 'I' comes from.

Visualize a homunculus if you like. Meaning a little man living inside of one's brain who watches the perceptions of the mind and processes the body's emotions. The guy in the brain who's supposed to be able to drive the body like one drives a car. Now envision this little man looking down into the torso of the body, which can be seen as the friendly house or 'homie' the man lives inside, and talking to the feminine soul, and you have the basic setup of Tupac's song. Tupac himself uses imagery to evoke this notion of the homunculus in 'Letter To The President' (off *Still I Rise*) when he says, 'Somewhere in the middle of my mind/ Is a nigga on a tightrope, screamin' 'Let 'em die.'' We argue that all the famous images of the Buddha yab yum body, which expresses the united masculine and feminine principles, show this basic setup of the man in head looking down at the feminine principle or spirit within the body.

So the 'I,' the little man in the head, met the feminine spirit who lives in the torso through his 'homie' or his house that is like a friend. Through his entire body. But, as Tupac's song says, there's a problem with this Cartesian setup. The soul doesn't want to be trapped in this identity prison because it's not a soul. It's skandalouz or is the skandhas in their wrathful form, which is why this female in the song is acting like she doesn't know the speaker. Why she's angry, deceitful, and disrespectful. There is discord between mind and body.

While Tupac delivers his next bar, Dillinger works in another significant sound effect. The second line in Tupac's first verse is 'So disappointed cause baby that shit was so phony,' and right after Tupac says 'phony,' Dillinger produces the sound of a rattlesnake. This sound certainly coincides with a surface-level reading of the girl as deceptive because typically (and definitely biblically) snakes are metaphors for trickery and deceit. However, in Hindu-Buddhist circles, the snake is often associated with the spine or the coiled 'feminine' kunda energy gathered at its base, which is closely affiliated with the skandhas because the spine is considered the bridge of communication between the outside world, the body, and the mind – the convergence point where the skandhas heap or aggregate. In Kundalini yoga, the objective is for the participant to get the coiled snake energy at the base of the spine to unwind and climb upward along the backbone and into the head. This is why Daz Dillinger's rattlesnake sound effect in 'Skandalouz' directly follows Tupac's phrase 'phony.'

On a surface level, while we recognize that 'phony' means fake, and there certainly is something fake about the shadow-anima when Tupac's speaker first encounters her in her 'corpse' form, we also argue that 'phony' here is an aural pun that figures the spine as a 'phone' or cord of communication between the skandhas and consciousness. In a lecture on Tantric Buddhism, British philosopher and theologian Alan Watts also compares Kundalini yoga and its Buddhist continuation, Tantra, to a phone call made to the divine (about which we'll have more to say in a later chapter.) It is from the position of the head or consciousness that the speaker in 'Skandalouz' approaches their feminine aggregate as though looking and speaking down through the body to its anima or 'skandha.' According to Buddhist reasoning, 'skandha' is always met through 'one's homie' or body because 'skandha' is not only the internally 'trapped' material of the outside world (like food) but is also the internally captured outside world in the form of sense data that comprise perceptions. Because one can perceive the outside only from within, it's always through the body that one meets the outside in the only form through which the outside can be known – skandha. Furthermore, skandha is always 'phony' not only because the outside passes through the body's senses and travels up the phone-cord-like spine before consciousness can perceive it. Skandha is always also 'phony' because 'she's' always an impression, perception, simulacrum, or ideal of the 'real world.' Similar to the distinction between noumenon and phenomenon in the philosophy of Immanuel Kant, a thing in itself can never be fully known. It is always inferred because the thing in itself must pass through the mediation of the senses and so is never noumenon proper but is always phenomenon or mental perception.

Tupac's 'Skandalouz,' we argue, in the simplest of terms, maps the speaker's progression through Jung's individuation stages, from persona-stage to Self-stage. In other words, the speaker moves from one's confused dividedness wherein ego consciousness identifies with persona while the unconscious identifies with the anima (thus creating an addictive and ultimately insatiable dependence on women) to the 'final' plateau of individuation when one 'becomes woman' or a masculine-feminine Whole Self capable of difference production. This shift is evident in the play between the following lines from Tupac's track:

> While you proceed with precision, you had the table hosed
> No, I ain't mad at you, baby, go 'head and play them fools
> They chose not to listen
> So now he's stuck inside his house and can't leave without his bitch permission
> The mission's to be a playa, my alias is Boss
> Drop the top on these jealous niggaz, playa let me floss.

Because those at the persona stage of masculinity 'chose not to listen' to their inner anima in its rawest and most unconscious state of potentiality, they get stuck inside their 'house' or their own body in its persona-anima deadlock. These persona-men are, like Jung says, slaves both to the woman within and the woman without, and they can leave neither their literal houses nor their figurative houses or bodies without permission from their own policing ideals.

Contrary to this state of internalized oppression, however, the speaker in 'Skandalouz' says outright, 'The mission's to be a... Boss.' This mission to 'be a Boss' is to be what Jung would call a 'Whole Self.' The mission is to be able to have a 'drop-top' vehicle/ body, meaning not only to vertically drop all that is repressed and held high down and out through that which is low, but to channel the low up and out through a roofless top. As mentioned in the introduction, the image of decapitation (a 'vehicle' without a top) is a sacred symbol of liberation in Hinduism. Kali decapitates and thereby subjugates 'Shiva' over and over because, in this configuration, he represents her ego ideal or the repressed skandhas she perpetually sheds. Shiva himself, figured similarly, is frequently represented with the 'sacred water' of the 'Ganges' flowing from the top of his head. This low-to-high, vertical ascent of discharging energies is what Tupac depicts with the line, 'Drop the top on these jealous niggaz, playa let me floss.' To 'floss,' in this sense, is to fully integrate the anima into one's consciousness so that the skandhas can openly flow through the liberated body or 'drop top,' like floss through teeth – fresh and reborn over and over.

This self-expressive act of 'flossing' the skandhas is figured as economic for Tupac and the Hindus. The persona-man, forever unconsciously chained to his dead shadow-anima, is in a schizophrenic bind. While he strives to domesticate his anima and overpower 'her' so that he can be 'Clyde Barrow' to whichever external woman he's trying to frame as his 'Bonnie Parker,' he's always setting himself up to endure what Freud terms the 'return of the repressed,' where (in this instance and in Jungian terms) the held-down anima comes back and figuratively castrates and demasculinizes the man over and over. In 'Skandalouz,' similar to Hinduism, this demasculinization is figured as 'robbing' the man of his 'money.' Regarding this, the speaker in 'Skandalouz' says:

> It's scandalous
> I never liked your backstabbin ass, trick
> Used to watch your money grabbin, who you baggin bitch?

The anima is associated with the back ('backstabbin ass'), which is not only figuratively what is repressed behind one's eyes or in the back of one's mind but, in the Hindu system, is also literally where the feminine zone, or yoni, is located. Similar to Hinduism, the above quote from 'Skandalouz' figures the shadow-anima as stealing currency from the persona-man from behind his back.

Currency, in Hinduism, is sometimes connected to sexual power, virility, and semen. In "'Semen Contains Vitality and Heredity, Not Germs': Seminal Discourse in the AIDS Era," Khal *et al.* make the argument that HIV prevention programs in South Asia aren't effective because they ignore the sexual health concerns of men within that cultural framework. We quote only the section describing the Hindu idea that semen and money are connected, as it's what pertains to our argument here, the understanding being that semen is one key aspect of the repressed skand(h)as that comprise the ego ideal in the form of the shadow-anima:

> Men in this study also referred to semen as *dhatu*. The word *dhatu* also means 'vital essence' which is analogous to *birjo*. The Bangla word *birjo* used to mean semen. They also used the word *mal* (valuable goods) to indicate semen. Thus, the symbolic meaning of *birjo* is wealth and power

of men... Bangladeshi men traditionally equate monetary wealth with manhood and sexual potency. To emphasize the significance of semen in the life of men, traditional practitioners in India use the following metaphor that 'a poor man who has no money' is similar to 'a sexually weak person who has no semen.'

As shown, weakness and the loss of semen are synonymous in Hindu culture. Therefore, a repressed or shadow-anima or a lodged and congealed skandha can easily be perceived as both a lack of health and a lack of money.

Jung's anima and animus, distinctly, are purely psychic phenomena. Persona-man, in Jung, psychically assigns his repressed unconscious a feminine role. This is a valuable framework because we know that when Jung talks about the anima and addresses the final stage of the individuation process that he terms 'becoming woman' he isn't speaking about real women but is rather accounting for the psychic makeup of man. In Hinduism, in general, and Kundalini yoga, specifically, the imperative is for the 'male' aspect of self to empower his neglected or impoverished feminine side, thereby maximizing the man's vitality, destroying the shadow, and liberating the anima that will usher in one's experience of the collective unconscious (and the case is similar with *Kabbalah*, which we'll look at in a later chapter). With 'Skandalouz,' Tupac does something similar but approaches the problem from a different angle, with different consequences. The woman in 'Skandalouz,' like the one in Hinduism, is neglected or impoverished: 'My sister precious in poverty.'

Whereas in the Hindu system, the feminine aspect of self is frequently figured as 'wife,' Tupac's speaker refers to his 'anima' as 'sister,' not unlike the Egyptian system, where characters metaphorically embody both sibling and spouse. For example, Osiris' feminine half, Isis (known as 'the throne upon which he sits'), is represented simultaneously as his wife and twin sister. The figurative 'sister' of the speaker in Tupac's 'Skandalouz,' however, is not only poor. She's a thief: 'This bitch'll have ya wakin up with all your cash missin'.' This feature adds to the Hindu account something similar to Jung's description of the shadow-anima's ability to enslave persona-man. 'She's' not only lacking – she, in this neglected state, places the man's 'financial security' in jeopardy.

The speaker in 'Skandalouz,' we can then infer, will continue to start their day over and over again wanting empowerment because he does not understand that he is the 'female' he's unable to control and that he needs to care for his neglected aspect as though he were both paternal parent to his veiled femininity and his own fantasy dream lover. Moreover, Tupac makes it clear that there is an ambiguous connection between the sister and the speaker in 'Skandalouz' when the speaker says:"

> I'm askin', as if I'm qualified to analyze
> You're lookin at a bitch who specialize in tellin lies.

These lines do a lot. The first line, 'I'm askin', as if I'm qualified to analyze,' blurs the boundary between the speaker and his 'sister' by effectively saying *it takes one to know one*. Written in the second person, the second line, 'You're lookin at a bitch who specialize in tellin lies,' not only makes it possible to now read Tupac as the unreliable narrator of a 'bitch' to whom the line refers, because the reader's focus is directed toward him – it also redirects the listener's attention inward to an internal conflict within the listener, between the listener and their anima(us).

At this point, we need to pause to further flesh out how it is that the 'bitch' in the line 'You're looking at a bitch who specialize in tellin lies' can both refer not only to Tupac as the 'bitch' without but also, more importantly, to the listener's own 'bitch' within. To do so, we need to tap into the long philosophical tradition of addressing this phenomenon of 'inner deception.' There are a variety of secondary texts to which we could turn to aid us in laying a foundation for this problem of 'looking.' Because the Ancient Greek philosopher Plato is one of the oldest, the most lucid, and because we know he's a thinker Tupac studied, we turn to Plato's famous 'Allegory of the Cave.'

In 'Allegory of the Cave,' from *The Republic*, Plato describes a dialogue between his teacher Socrates and another student intellectual named Glaucon. In this dialogue, Socrates distinguishes between humans who are 'enlightened' and those who are 'unenlightened.' The critical block preventing the unenlightened from reaching enlightenment in 'Allegory of the Cave' is human sight and its close ties to human perception. According to Socrates, there is a fundamental flaw in human perception, and if this flaw in sight is known and corrected, humankind can be empowered to 'act rationally.' If it isn't, humanity will be a prisoner of its own illusions and misperceptions:

> Behold! Human beings living in an underground den, which has a mouth open towards the light and reaching all along the den; here they have been from their childhood, and have their legs and necks chained so that they cannot move, and can see only before them, being prevented by the chains from turning round their heads. Above and behind them a fire is blazing at a distance, and between the fire and the prisoners there is a raised way; and you will see, if you look, a low wall built along the way, like the screen which marionette players have in front of them, over which they show the puppets.

After describing this allegorical scenario where prisoners are chained at their backs in a cave and made to face what's effectively a movie screen made possible by fire and shadows, Socrates then explicitly tells Glaucon that 'the prison-house is the world of sight,' that the problem with the unenlightened is that 'they see only their own shadows, and that the process of enlightenment is at first a painful process. It's important to note that Plato's shadows are like false perceptions or illusions, whereas, for Jung, the shadow world is more like the repressed, unconscious drives behind illusion or the marionettes who are putting on Plato's shadow show. The reader can infer from Plato that the basic problem confronting the slave of misperception is that he can only see the product of sight and not the process whereby sight is brought into being. He literally and figuratively faces forward and cannot redirect his vision and energy inward and backward. Not only is the prisoner's vision in Plato's cave limited, but the limitation of his vision is also a by-product of the limitation experienced throughout his whole body. He is 'fronting' and so lacks a depth of understanding both about his own body and his own cognitive processes. It should be noted, however, that Plato is an idealist. He sees the world of material reality as an illusion. We, following Buddhism and Tupac, feel that Plato goes too far and thus take his allegory in the opposite direction. The repressed skandhas are the source of deception. The idea of individuality is deceptive. Independence is deceptive. And, certainly, 'everything is an illusion' insofar as ideas and bodies and civilizations come and go just like (along the lines of geologic time) mountains and valleys come and go, but, as far as we're concerned, reality isn't a simulation generated by the mind of God or something like that.

For us, the fire that burns behind the slave of Plato's cave and casts shadows on the wall refers to the sense data the body captures, which, as shadow, both plays like a film for the mind and projects onto the outside world. The idea here is that an enlightened person knows that when seeing they are both seeing 'shadows' – images caused by sense data and/or the continually produced stream of memories and fantasies – at the same time their eye is capturing new, raw data. The awakened individual knows then that they have to question their own vision and perception of the world because it's tainted not only by past perceptions but also by social conditioning. They know that their brain works, to a lesser or greater degree of extremity, on a delay separate from real-time, which is never fully accessible. Like someone slipping into a zone when driving their car, it's only after they ask themselves, 'How the hell did I get from the last stoplight to this one?' do they recognize real-time. This state of absolute presence.

The problem of projecting the past onto the present has a wide array of possible adverse outcomes. To provide a simple but tragic real-life example, a white police officer who stereotypes a black motorist and so winds up shooting an innocent man is a textbook example of the dangers of not being cognizant of one's own visual apparatus. This ignorant officer encounters a hostile black criminal on Monday and then meets a law-abiding black male citizen on Tuesday. Because the officer isn't aware of how his body, brain, and perceptions work, he wrongly carries forward and re-projects the dangerous black man from Monday onto the body of the innocent black man he encounters on Tuesday. This is textbook stereotyping, and the result is that another innocent African American person is murdered (see Black Lives Matter for a dizzying array of further examples and sad details). Had the officer known that, in the words of Tupac, he wasn't actually looking at a real person in front of him but was rather looking at 'a bitch who specialize in tellin lies,' or his own shadow, he would have been able to check himself before approaching an innocent man and murdering him.

The whole problematic that is the 'Allegory of the Cave' is the premise for Tupac's track 'Starin Through My Rear View.' Here, like Walter Benjamin's angel of history who looks backward at the debris of the past while being propelled forward into a direction they cannot see, Tupac recasts the slave staring at shadows in Plato's cave scene as a 'black man' (figuratively the one dwelling in the darkness within) looking at the world through the rearview mirror of his automobile (metaphorical body):

> I'm seeing nothin but my dreams comin true?
> While I'm starin at the world through my rearview
> They got me.

The line 'They got me' casts an ominous tone over these lines and suggests, as does the police brutality described in the rest of the song, that the man is trapped in a perceptual feedback loop or a gaze of and for a self-fulfilling prophecy. Even while looking forward, he's always looking backward and so lives an utterly homogeneous existence where tomorrow is made into yesterday ad infinitum.

The specific problem Tupac addresses in 'Skandalouz,' however, like Jung's problem, is the problem of persona-man projecting the shadow-anima onto a real woman or a series of real women with adverse effects. With the lyric 'You're looking at a bitch who specialize in tellin lies,' Tupac directly cautions his listener and encourages them to pay attention to their own inherent flaw of sight because the lying 'bitch' they're looking at isn't only some woman who exists outside themselves but is also their own repressed shadow-anima. They're always seeing the outside through their 'rearview mirror.'

Another facet that makes Tupac's work with the shadow archetype so politically unique is how he racializes it, or, rather, how he highlights that through social conditioning the shadow is always being racialized. Tupac knows that the philosophical history of conceptualizing one's own veiled interiority as a black shadow and the history of racial oppression in the world aren't mutually exclusive. They are two realities that sometimes overlap and sometimes do not, and, in addition to the fact that they very much are historical realities, they are also socially conditioned and malleable. People psychically associate their own insides as shadows because they can't immediately see inside themselves. They close their eyes to look within, and all they see is blackness and traces of light they don't understand. They hear voices and think thoughts they're scared to admit to themselves, much less to others. Manipulative governing bodies and their intellectual elites bent on creating ideologies to justify their racist, territorial agendas know people are frightened by their own alienated shadow selves. So they racialize and colorize 'the shadow.' Then they direct people's fear of themselves outward onto people of color to exploit the societies under their influence and control. In other words, they racialize the shadow to dominate and extract from both so-called people of color and so-called whites.

In "What Carl Jung Said About Race Relations in America," religious studies professor, social worker, and Jungian analyst Michael Gellert argues that for America to confront its pernicious race problem head-on, individuals must first deal with their racial complexes:

> It was to our dissociated parts that Jung was referring when he said, 'every [American] Negro has a white complex and every [white] American a Negro complex.'... The white complex is, figuratively speaking, the white man inside the black person's psyche, as the black complex is the black man inside the white person's psyche. The white complex operates in the African-American psyche as a judgmental and alienating authority principle that compels African-Americans to displace onto whites their inner authority and the measuring rod of their own goodness. The black complex operates in the white American psyche as a threatening instinctual force – what Joseph Conrad called the 'African within' – compelling white Americans to displace onto blacks their animal nature, dark fears (such as fear of death), and evil impulses... In most of the myths, legends, and folk tales of the hero, there is a confrontation between the hero and a 'wholly other,' some monster, evil figure, or antagonist who threatens him or tests his worth and abilities. From a psychological point of view, the 'wholly other' is really within the hero himself... [T]he heroic challenge of race relations in America (is really)... a confrontation with oneself.

Tupac often refused to present himself as 'himself' and instead chose to embody and perform the repressed shadow to challenge listeners to confront 'him' and integrate 'him' into their conscious lives. In 'Hail Mary,' Tupac says, 'When they turn out the lights, I'll be there in the dark/ Thuggin eternal through my heart.' In 'Late Night,' Tupac states explicitly, 'Nobody knows me I'm a shadow/ Army fatigues made for battle, pockets fulla ammo.' The track 'Can't C Me' begins with the lyrics:

> The blind stares of a million pairs of eyes
> Lookin hard but won't realize
> They can never see the P.

In 'What Carl Jung Said About Race Relations in America,' Gellert argues that the more 'white society' alienates themselves from their own shadow selves while simultaneously projecting their shadows onto 'African Americans,' the more 'white society' pressures 'African Americans' to either consciously or unconsciously become the advocates of the repressed aspects of humanity that 'white society' can't psychically accept. Gellert states:

> *By having unconsciously projected all this* [fear] *upon blacks, whites have in fact become what they most fear in blacks: barbaric and diabolically dark.* And yet, the more whites condemn and push this side of their psyche away, the more it is forced to live itself out through the African American... The problems from which African Americans suffer and which invariably affect the rest of society – poverty, unemployment, drug abuse, violence and crime – are basically symptoms or ways through which the dissociated part of the white American psyche returns to obtain recognition and redemption.

Tupac never had a problem being the bad guy everyone schizophrenically loved and hated, the spokesperson for polyamory, drugs, and self-indulgence, and his commitment to his bodhisattva-thug-life mission was one designed to get others to accept these aspects in themselves so they could finally see that he was more than the sum of his game, that he was truly enlightened.

Tupac wanted people to see not only the enlightened African in him. He wanted people to see the 'blackness.' And he wanted them to see it in themselves. In a speech Tupac gave at the Malcolm X Grassroots Movement in 1992, Tupac said:

> It's not just the white man that's keeping us trapped. It's [also] black.

> And we have to find the new African in everybody... But before we can be African, we gotta be black first... In our striving to be enlightened, we forgot about all our brothers in the street, about all our dope dealers, our pushers and our pimps, and that's who's teaching the next generation. Because y'all not doing it.

Accepting 'blackness' – and all its symbolic, shadowy negativity – is an essential step in the process of enlightenment for Tupac. And the acceptance of 'blackness,' along with the discovery of 'the new African,' isn't just a pivotal stage for individuals with a high amount of melanin in their skin. It's something to be found and work to be done within everyone.

Tupac moves in a different direction than Gellert in suggesting that not only do whites need to integrate their own repressed black other but that blacks need to as well. Tupac composed and made his compositions available to both white and black listeners, and, among those two groups, Tupac makes it overtly clear through his lyrics that he loved black people in a special way and so thereby crafted his tracks to be received by the black community in a special way. Yet, in Tupac's whole body of work, the primarily alienated other that is offered to listeners to integrate into themselves is the repressed black shadow that is 'Tupac.' That said, Tupac, at times, also does something along the lines of encouraging black people to confront their 'white complex' and integrate those aspects of themselves historically and racistly associated with white society. In a 1991 promotional interview recorded not long after Tupac released his debut album *2Pacalypse Now*, Tupac states,

> Let's be realistic. Just like it wasn't white people that beat me down in Oakland. It was two white cops. Two white, crooked cops. That's what that was. We have to be more realistic about our enemies. It's easy to say 'white folks is evil.' That's easy. But then you're leading us into more of a slaughter because we're gonna find out all whites ain't evil.

Tupac clearly understood that if you take the stereotype of 'blackness' and the stereotype of 'whiteness' and you add them together, you get something like a whole human being (or the whole range of human potential) and that any philosophy that tries to alienate the one from the other is flawed.

No album exemplifies this tenet in Tupac to get blacks to confront their 'white complex' like *Me Against the World*. The following are lyrics from the track 'Heavy in the Game:'

> Quit trying to be an O.G. and pay your dues
> If you choose to apply yourself, go with the grain
> Then come the riches and the bitches and the fame
> Heavy in the game/ The game's been good to me.

Also from *Me Against the World*, here is dialogue from the end of 'Young Niggaz':

> Stay strong, nigga. You could be a fuckin' accountant, not a dope dealer. You know what I'm sayin'? Go to school, nigga. Go to school. Fuck around, and you pimpin out here, you could be a lawyer – real dough. Niggas gotta get they priorities straight.

The virtues of following the rules, practicing self-discipline, maintaining school attendance, and prioritizing, sadly, are often mistakenly perceived to be associated with the persona of whiteness. Tupac clearly wanted black youth to accept and realize their own capacity to be focused in these ways as much as he strived to get people to accept their figurative 'darkness.'

All the same, color in Tupac can, at times, be very much a polysemic signifier that doesn't refer to race at all. Whether he accessed this tradition through Jung, who spent a great deal of time studying Taoism and its color-coded yin-yang logic, through the spiritual culture Leila Steinberg exposed him to, or just through the esoteric 'backstreets' of mystical encryptions and inferences, color, for Tupac, can make distinctions between the problematic binary of unenlightened and enlightened as much as it can signify whiteness and blackness. Take, for example, a text we know Tupac read: St. John of the Cross' *Dark Night of the Soul* (which we'll have much more to say about in a later chapter). In brief summation, *Dark Night of the Soul* gives an account of Jung's individuation process through the narrative of the feminine soul's marriage to God, who, in the vein of the Old Testament's *Song of Songs,* is masculinized and figured as the Bridegroom to the soul, which is figured as Bride. The person who is a beginner on the road that is the 'dark night' initially perceives the light that they find within to be the guiding light of God, but then God shuts off the light and turns off the water in the body, which is figured as a house:

> When they are going about these spiritual exercises with the greatest delight and pleasure, and when they believe that the sun of Divine favor is shining most brightly upon them, God turns all this light of theirs into darkness, and shuts against them the door and the source of the sweet spiritual water which they were tasting in God...

Every time we encounter this quote from *Dark Night of the Soul* in the context of thinking about Tupac, we can't help but recall Tupac's line from 'Hail Mary': 'When they turn off the lights, I'll be there in the dark/ Thuggin eternal through my heart,' where Tupac's voice is figured as that of God. But, more to our point about color, in *Dark Night of the Soul*, the ultimate imperative for the practitioner is to move from the light to the dark. Darkness is the end goal and the marker of a more mature union with God. In other words, darkness is the true light. In *Dark Night of the Soul*, St. John relays and appropriates St. Dionysius' term 'a ray of darkness' to highlight this fact. Therefore, in St. John of the Cross, to become dark is to merge with God.

Knowing that Tupac was influenced by *Dark Night of the Soul* and that darkness is equivalent to enlightenment in St. John of the Cross' text, we argue that, at times, Tupac's lyrics can be interpreted similarly. But, for Tupac, we suggest that, sometimes, light also becomes white and dark becomes black. From the album *Makaveli*, early on in the song 'White Man's World,' Tupac speaks the lines:

> Nothin' but love for you, my sister. Might even know how hard it is. No doubt. Bein' a woman, a black woman at that. No doubt. Shit. In this white man's world.

Without even lingering on the fact that these lines can be read so that 'black,' 'woman' and 'shit' run parallel and how that speaks back to and connects with the Buddhist notion of the skandhas that not only have negative but also have very positive connotations, we want to pause to focus on the lines 'Might even know how hard it is. No doubt. Bein' a woman, a black woman at that.' This is a consistent aspect of Tupac's lyrical genius, a little moment somewhere in a song that throws a bomb across the rest of the track, if not his whole œuvre, and thereby defies conventional interpretation. By stating at the beginning of 'White Man's World' that he 'might even know' the experience of being a 'black woman,' and then doubling back to say 'no doubt' that he does in fact know, Tupac problematizes how the reader interprets both 'womanhood' and 'blackness' not only throughout this track but through all of his work. Now when we listen to 'Ghetto Gospel' and Tupac's line 'It ain't about black or white cause we human/ I hope we see the light before it's ruined,' we are forced to wonder if, in the way that in St. John of the Cross enlightenment is both the marriage of the feminine and the masculine as well as the light and the dark, Tupac's human is simultaneously black and white, masculine and feminine, unenlightened and enlightened.

Something similar can be said for all of Tupac's work and its use of gender and color. Take the song 'Str8 Ballin',' off *Thug Life: Vol 1*, which begins with Tupac saying, 'I would share the definition of ballin' with you white folks, but no. The game is to be sold and not told, so fuck you.' The fact that Tupac chooses to spell 'straight ballin' with the number 8 – typically associated with a figure eight, a Mobius strip, and infinity – when placed within the framework of this polysemic color logic we've been unfolding, makes interpreting the 'white folks' here a conundrum. To be 'white,' we're suggesting, can be read as being half of a whole or unenlightened. Something that can apply to anyone despite their skin color. For clarity's sake, this isn't to suggest that Tupac doesn't also position himself as a historically codified 'black person' or 'African American' and that he doesn't address historically codified 'white people', because he does. This certainly seems to be the most literal way of reading '16 On Death Row' off *R U Still Down (Remember Me)*, where Tupac's speaker is a young man sentenced to die in prison:

> And to my homies out buryin' motha fuckers
> Steer clear of these Aryan motha fuckers
> 'Cause once they got you locked up, they got you trapped

You're better off gettin shot up.

Whether the historical race category 'Aryan' refers to all 'white people' or whether it evokes the Nazi use of the term and thereby refers only to racist whites is open to interpretation. Notwithstanding, our point is that while we recognize that approaching these lines literally isn't the only way of approaching them, we also recognize that a literal interpretation is valid. That said, we strongly suggest that there are moments in Tupac where he uses racial markers like black and white in unconventional, creative ways. In ways that signify a more universal distinction between the 'enlightened' and the 'unenlightened,' problematic though that distinction may be because of elitism and a whole other set of issues we won't fully get into here.

Yab Yum.

Skanda Muruga.

Carl Jung.

Friedrich Nietzsche

Chapter 2

Tupac's Sacred Biotech

'Caring for myself is not self-indulgence, it is self-preservation, and that is an act of political warfare.'

Audre Lorde, 'A Burst of Light'

According to German psychoanalyst Carl Gustav Jung, not only can one metaphorically become a woman to achieve the complete status of a Whole Self (a female-male-difference-generator), but one can also undergo a conjoining with technology to do so. Before one can take this step, however, one must first recognize oneself as lacking, incomplete, and castrated.

Tupac had an unfortunate leg up on most in this regard because in 1994, in the lobby of Quad Recording Studios, Tupac was almost literally castrated as one of the five bullets he took from a shooting he believed was orchestrated by Biggie Smalls and Sean Combs hit him in the testicles. Tupac describes the injury in an interview with Kevin Powell:

> I opened my pants, and I could see the gunpowder and the hole in my Karl Lani drawers. I didn't want to pull them down to see if my dick was still there. I just saw a hole and went, 'Oh shit. Roll me some weed.

Following the understanding that one is castrated, for C.G. Jung, one can then and only then turn to what he frames as technology to facilitate 'Wholeness.' For Jung, technology is the employment of 'the natural gradient [of life] for the performance of work.' (63-4). A beaver dam is an example Jung turns to in order to explain this phenomenon. While the river has a natural gradient, the dam blocks the river and thus allows for a variety of power redistributions that wouldn't be possible otherwise, not only for the beaver but for all who live in that ecosystem.

This chapter analyzes Tupac as a sacred cyborg – both man and the machine he uses to help deconstruct rigid skandhas that form into oppressive ideal egos. To look at Tupac through this frame, we turn to the album *All Eyez On Me*, released following Tupac's incarceration, specifically, the track 'Heartz of Men.' Speaking to Death Row Records CEO Suge Knight and producer DJ Quik, in 'Heartz of Men,' Tupac says,

> Hay Suge, what I tell you nigga when I come outta jail what I was gonna do? I was gonna start digging into these niggas chests, right? Watch this. Hay, Quik, let me see them binoculars, nigga. The binoculars.

We argue, here, that the 'binoculars' Tupac references aren't literal binoculars but are instead figurative biotech for looking at exactly what the title suggests the song is an inquiry into: the heart, inside, or the epicenter of mankind.

This kind of directional reversal coupled with a machinic reference isn't out of character for Shakur. In the song 'How Do You Want It,' also off *All Eyez On Me*, Tupac says, 'I'm hitting switches on bitches like I've been fixed with hydraulics.' Tupac's 'switches' (or linguistic reversals), along with his thematically suturing himself in his songs with machines, are the inquiry of this chapter. To establish the context within which Tupac is working here, let us be clear that our research into sacred texts as a genre suggests that figurative assemblages linking humans and machines aren't unusual. Meaning, within the framework of not only Jung but also spiritual texts more broadly, the idea of the body conjoining with the materiality of tech to facilitate awakening is a recurring motif, whether it be the Buddha's begging bowl, the boat of Ra, the water well Christ stands beside as he converses with a Samaritan woman, or the trumpet that brought down the walls of Jericho. Joseph Campbell elucidates that religion means to 'link back,' and so, in this light, the study of religion is the study of various links and linking methodologies. For Tupac and those thinkers we will turn to in order to aid us in clarifying Tupac's position, these links are more materialistic and literal than one might presuppose, and they are very much machinic.

In Jung's work *Psychic Energy*, Jung argues that technology bridges the gap between the conscious self and one's unconscious potential in the form of surplus libido. For Jung, psychic energy works like and is its own kind of physical energy system (20). Observing the connection between body and mind, Jung argues that psychic energy is part of a more extensive, biological energy system, not separate from it. Distinct from Freud, who thinks of the libido only in terms of sexual energy, Jung's definition of libido is more all-encompassing of vital, life energy in general (32). Jung's libidinal energy follows a natural gradient and works by way of opposing forces that generate difference or life by firing off one another. However, that natural oscillation can be temporarily offset to produce work through a process that Jung calls 'canalization.' Jung refers to the technology capable of enacting the canalization process as 'psychic mechanisms':

> In the same way that the living body as a whole is a machine, other adaptations to physical and chemical conditions have the value of machines that make other forms of transformation possible... Just as man has succeeded in inventing a turbine, and, by conducting a flow of water to it, in transforming the latter's kinetic energy into electricity capable of manifold applications, so he has succeeded, with the help of a psychic mechanism, in converting natural instincts, which would otherwise follow their gradient without performing work, into other dynamic forms that are productive of work.

Not only is the whole body a living machine capable of making machines that affect one's environment and so inadvertently affect oneself, but the body is also capable of manufacturing psychic – which isn't to say immaterial – mechanisms that immediately convert libidinal energy into work. The definition of work Jung uses here is a physics definition. Work, in the discipline of physics, refers to the transfer of energy to an object. In this instance, Jung is talking about the transfer of energy to an object that then will be allowed to act as the catalyst for the binary-libidinal machine capable of work production, including the most important task one's work can be directed toward – the journey of individuation or enlightenment.

Jung's libidinal energy, which works by way of opposing forces, can also, either intentionally or unintentionally, be offset so dramatically that rather than producing work, the canalization winds up deadlocking the entire body-mind mechanism:

> During the progression of libido the pairs of opposites are united in the co-ordinated flow of psychic processes. Their working together makes possible the balanced regularity of these processes, which without this inner polarity would become one-sided and unreasonable.

Difference and gestation are necessary components of life because once one side of what we call Jung's *binary-libidinal-machine* shuts down, 'positive and negative can no longer unite in co-ordinated action, because both have attained an equal value which keeps the scales balanced.' Balance is not good here, as it implies entropy, the absence of movement, or the nonexistence of freedom.

According to Jung, regression is an immediate corollary of an individual's adapting to their outer, sociopolitical environment (60). Because '[l]ibido moves not only forwards and backwards, but also outwards and inwards,' regression occurs when one neglects their inner-self and increasingly becomes a persona to conform to the norms of society and work to the benefit of the dominant order (62). Tupac knew what it meant to be pressured into losing his humanity and being an exclusively machine-persona all too well:

> There's a machine that I have nothing to do with. It's called the 'Tupac Machine.' And the media in this county has fueled it and made me a monster.

Jung explains, however, that regression can also come about from the individuation process itself:

> Regression, on the other hand, as an adaptation to the conditions of the inner world, springs from the vital need to satisfy the demands of individuation. Man is not a machine in the sense that he can consistently maintain the same output of work. He can meet the demands of outer necessity... only if he is also adapted to his own inner world... Conversely, he can only adapt to his inner world and achieve harmony with himself when he is adapted to the environmental conditions.

By turning inward and striving to integrate the unconscious into one's conscious reality, one can go so far into the interior that the exterior is completely neglected. One thus inadvertently tips the scales of their binary-libidinal machine and coagulates excess energy onto one side or a single part of a whole that then refuses to redistribute and so brings about a complete entropic malfunction.

Tupac's track 'Me and My Girlfriend,' from *The Don Killuminati: The 7 Day Theory* (released just two months after he died in 1996), deftly shows how the anima, once dredged out of the depths of the unconscious and brought into the light of waking consciousness, can be represented both as feminine and as a psychic mechanism capable of the canalization of libido. 'Me and My Girlfriend,' in the most basic and literal sense, is an encomium for Tupac's 'girlfriend.' But Tupac's 'girlfriend' in the track isn't a literal female. 'She's' a gun. The track picks up on a common theme in Tupac: deception and disloyalty. Tupac unequivocally argues in 'Me and My Girlfriend' that the only 'girl' he can count on to be consistent is his 'gun.' Denotatively, all females (if not all other people in general) cannot be trusted. We, however, argue that the 'gun' in Tupac's song is connotatively a cipher for what Jung terms a psychic mechanism.

The first indication that Tupac is a 'Whole Self,' in the Jungian sense that 'Whole' means a male-female-assemblage or enlightened individual who has undergone the individuation process and is thereby full of potential and open to difference, comes through in the very beginning of the track. The opening lyrics of the song are spoken by a female voice (rapper Virginya Slim), who says,

> Shit, you mother fucking right
> I'm the bitch who's keeping it live and keeping it hot when you punk ass niggas don't.

Following Virginya Slim's part, Tupac says, 'Look for me.' By beginning 'Me and My Girlfriend' with the imperative for the listener to look for Tupac right after the female voice says, 'I'm the bitch who's keeping it live and keeping it hot,' listeners are invited to perceive an overlap between Tupac's 'me' and Virginya Slim's 'I,' suggesting that 'she' is the prize to be sought after.

Bracketing the wasteful 'shit,' its connection to the 'I,' and that figure's connections to the Buddhist concept of the skandhas to the side (already analyzed in the previous chapter), we not only want to highlight the fluidity of the transition between Virginya Slim's 'I' and Tupac's 'me' to further support our claim they work together in a more literal sense than might be assumed – we also argue that there is something divine about the 'girlfriend' in the track, highlighting that not only is 'she' not a literal female but neither is she a literal 'gun' either. Regarding his 'girlfriend,' Tupac says,

> We closer than the hands of time
> Deeper than the drive of mankind.

Although they move at different speeds and sometimes point in different directions, the hands of time on a clock are connected, so to be 'closer than the hands of time,' if taken literally, is to be inextricable. This reading parallels the more-easily-assumed figurative one: being 'closer than the hands of time' just means something like having a solid friendship or relationship. Moving past the reading that interprets 'the drive of mankind' as the tool with which mankind drives, the lyric can also refer to human desire, so to have a connection that goes deeper than species desire itself is to have a link that precedes and thereby transcends humanity (the implication being that depth is frequently associated with both digressions in scale – into DNA and the molecular – as well as a move backward in time). Time so close that it closes in on itself. Thereby, similar to Christ, who, as God, comes before Adam and thereby bypasses original sin and thus also transcends his own humanity, these lyrics suggest not only a connection to something nonhuman within the human but a connection to a gestalt that ruptures temporal species classification.

For Jung, integrating the unconscious into one's conscious reality isn't only accepting one's veiled femininity. Integrating the anima into one's life is much more revolutionary because, even though the psyche tends to feminize the anima, 'she' isn't a literal female. Nor is she only an overlooked aspect of one's humanity. She is the gateway not only to the personal unconsciousness but also to the collective unconsciousness. To clarify and redefine what was reviewed in the previous chapter, there are two aspects of the unconscious for Jung, the personal and the collective. The personal unconscious is like a reserve for individual repression, a psychic trashcan or placeholder where the individual throws and stores anything that is too difficult for them to deal with or where they exile any desire or thought that would be considered contradictory to one's socially normalized persona. The collective unconscious, however, is a common space shared by all humans. For Jung, the collective unconscious is phylogenctic. It's the shared, evolutionary history of humanity's conscious mind that all humankind carries with them on a deep biological and psychic level:

> Just as the human body represents a whole museum of organs, each with a long evolutionary history behind it, so we should expect to find that the mind is organized in a similar way. It can no more be a product without history than is the body in which it exists. By 'history' I do not mean the fact that the mind builds itself up by conscious reference to the past through language and other cultural traditions. I am referring to the biological, prehistoric, and unconscious development of the mind in archaic man, whose psyche was still close to that of the animals.

For Jung, every human carries within himself the biologically historical record of the development of the human mind that goes so far into the past that it almost precedes humanity or comes 'close to that of the animals.' In 'Me and My Girlfriend,' Tupac goes a step further than Jung, suggesting that his relationship with his 'girlfriend' actually goes back before the development of the human species or is 'closer than the hands of time' and 'deeper than the drive of mankind.' Therefore, Tupac's 'girlfriend/ gun' can paradoxically be interpreted both as a gateway to the collective unconscious and as the collective unconscious itself, which, for

Tupac, is nonhuman.

In addition to being both feminized and indicated as something abstract, like a spirit or code that predates the emergence of the human race, the speaker's 'girlfriend' in Tupac's track is also represented as technology, namely a 'weapon', and more specifically a 'gun.' By focusing on the functionality of Tupac's 'gun' and its target or mark of attack, we suggest the quality of this apparatus will be more clearly divulged. In 'My and My Girlfriend,' Tupac states,

> Fuck'em all, watch 'em fall screamin
> Automatic gunfire exorcising all demons
> My Mafioso messiah
> My congregation high
> Ready to die
> We bail out
> Then take the jail back
> Niggas united.

The focal point of attack for Tupac's 'girlfriend/ gun' is established as demonic. Thus, the 'girlfriend/ gun's' objective isn't to target other humans but is rather to 'exorcise demons' or internal conflicts. The 'girlfriend/ gun' that executes this exorcism is referenced as Tupac's 'Mafioso messiah.' Put differently, 'she' is Tupac's gangster savior – all Tupac needs in 'this life of sin,' he says, is his 'girlfriend,' suggesting again that 'she' is not a literal gun but is something more like a sacred machine for laying waste to internal enemies, during internal battles. In Jungian terms, 'she' is a psychic mechanism for canalization insofar as the work derived from canalization is effectuated to the process of individuation.

The energy of Tupac's 'girlfriend/ gun' is, we argue, itself what Tupac is comparing to the collective unconscious. This, we suggest, is why 'she' can be figured simultaneously as 'collective unconscious' and machine. 'She' unreliably slips in and out between body, machine, the link between consciousness and unconsciousness, and sometimes figures the unconsciousness itself. Similarly, Tupac positions himself in these lines as a preacher with a congregation that is high and revolutionarily motivated to overwhelm the prison system ('My congregation high/

Ready to die/ We bail out/ Then take the jail back/ Niggas united'). But because the 'we' has already been troubled to the extent that it can be read as one rather than two – this 'closer than the hands of time' overlap between Tupac and the female who is simultaneously also machine and unconscious – the plurality of the congregation itself, not to mention the literality of the prison, is also made ambiguous. Additionally, this logic can be applied to the phrase 'Niggas united,' making listeners wonder whether an apostrophe is to be added when transcribing these lyrics or not. Is it 'Niggas united?' Or is it 'Nigga's united?' as in *this 'nigga' or man is united within himself.*

Before continuing our analysis of psychic mechanisms for canalization in Tupac, we want to linger for a moment on the chronology between the lyrics 'We bail out/ Then take the jail back/ Niggas('s) united', because the theme of release that comes through the 'bail out' is prevalent as a first step not only in Tupac but in esoteric sacred texts in general, suggesting that prior to the introduction of a psychic mechanism (the inner unity – 'Nigga's united' – that follows taking the jail back) a proper catharsis has to occur. As Angélique Maria Gabrielle Lalonde marks in her work "Embodying Asana in All New Places," cathartic yoga methods are all too often missed by Western yoga schools (and, we'd like to add, are also frequently overlooked by a literary analysis of sacred texts), resulting in 'a melding of equivalent sources of identification detached from their origins or past contexts of meaning and practice.' Of the techniques typically overlooked or not known by Western yoga schools, Angélique Maria Gabrielle Lalonde specifically names the shatkarmas, which, we will argue, are not only of the utmost importance but are also commonly alluded to in Tupac. *Thus Spoke Zarathustra*, in its brazen critique of idealism, gives one of the strongest speculations as to why cathartic methods similar to the shatkarmas of yoga are ignored and testifies as to why turning one's attention to the grimy core of one's earthly body should be celebrated when Nietzsche says,

> To despise the earthly hath your spirit been persuaded, but not your bowels: these, however, are the strongest in you! And now is your spirit ashamed to be at the service of your bowels, and goeth by-ways and lying

ways to escape its own shame.

Attention to the earth, to the bowels, is requisite for Nietzsche's Overman, the enlightened one who has gone over the 'mountain' and does not aspire to fly away from Earth into Heaven but instead makes his descent downward. Even in the West's many attempts to study and teach yoga, Western idealism misses the depths within that one must delve into to dismantle egocentrism.

In an article titled "Physiological Effect of *Kriyas*: Cleansing Techniques," from the *International Journal of Yoga*, Sanjib Kumar Patra describes the 'kriyas' or 'shatkarmas' of hatha yoga:

> There are three humors in the body: *Kapha* (phlegm), *Pitta* (bile), and *Vata* (wind). In Ayurveda and Yoga, they are called *Tridoshas*. There should be an equilibrium state between these three humors in the body. Imbalance... causes impairment or disorders... Physiologically, an effort needs to be made to remove the mucus blocking in the respiratory tracts, excess fats from the body, and excess gastric juice secretions from the stomach... In *Hatha Yoga*, there are six purification practices specifically designed for serving this purpose. They are *Kriyas* or *Shatkarmas*... When the different systems of the body have been purified, the overall result is that energy can flow through the body freely.

The body can be thrown into a state of volatility if it carries within it an excess of phlegm, bile, or gas, which is, essentially, yesterday materialized. Or, as Nietzsche says,

> Verily, my brethren, the spirit IS a stomach! Life is a well of delight, but to him in whom the ruined stomach speaketh, the father of affliction, all fountains are poisoned.

Spirit, for Nietzsche, similar to the Buddhist notion of the skandhas, is a stomach that, if neglected, poisons not only the whole body – 'all fountains' – but also the mind, as a poisoned stomach 'speaketh' or produces bad thoughts, possibly even auditory and visual hallucinations. The shatkarmas are the yogic methods for freeing the body of this excess prior to the meditative practices of channeling the kundalini energy not only from the base of the body into the crown and vice versa, but also from the back of the body to the front and vice versa. This yogic pathway and process of production called kundalini yoga, we suggest, is, in altered terms, a big part of what Jung refers to when he talks about the canalization of entropic libidinal energy when it is aligned toward individuation.

Hatha Yoga Pradipika is a touchstone, 15th-century Sanskrit text on hatha yoga, written by Svatmarama. In Hans-Ulrich Rieker's commentary on the shatkarma section in the 1992 translation, Rieker states that in addition to the dangers that come from a body too burdened with excess waste, an adequately cleaned body is itself a precarious thing because a detoxified body is a powerful body:

> These six practices, which cleanse the body, should be carefully kept secret because they induce numerous wonderful results and are therefore held in high esteem with the great yogis. Why this secretiveness? What are these 'wonderful results'? Imagine a man who uses a low-tension electrical gadget, which is attached by a transformer to high-power current. The current he uses is barely noticeable with the fingertips. With the transformer removed, he receives an electric shock. Exactly so is it here. The unclean nadis act as a transformer to the life stream so that nothing untoward can happen. When the nadis are clean, the effectiveness of prana is many times increased, and this can become dangerous.

The most commonly utilized and most widely alluded to shatkarms are, as Rieker explains, encrypted in secrecy due to the power they deliver to the yogi (due to this practice of secrecy, one can never tell if shatkarma instructions are to be taken literally or figuratively), and mudras are one of the ways yogis encode their secret teachings. In hatha yoga and Buddhism, for example, mudras are not only external hand and body postures meant to channel energy. They also symbolize internal methods of shatkarma. Bhumisparsha mudra, or the Buddha's 'earth touching gesture' (seen in many statues of the Buddha), symbolizes the Buddha's triumph over the demon Mara and his temptress daughters, as well as indicates to yogic practitioners the shatkarma of 'earth touching' (also known as being 'in touch' with one's feminine side, which isn't only a mental but is also very much a physical endeavor).

Like Christ and the Buddha, Tupac establishes his own mudras and alludes to shatkarma in various instances. The multiple images of Tupac with his middle finger up or his fingers formed into the shape of a gun pointed at his head (reminding us of the famous photograph of the infamous Tantra teacher Chogyam Trungpa) come to mind. Like the images of Christ or the Buddha, where the enlightened one will have one hand down while the other is up or one hand holding an object while the other is open, the well-known image of Tupac, pistol tucked in pants, holding up the middle finger with one hand (a shatkarma mudra if there ever was one) while he pinches a blunt in the other is possibly the most iconic.

Thinking on shatkarma mudras, the shatkarmas themselves, and how they connect to Jung's psychic mechanisms while keeping with our analysis, Tupac says in 'Me and My Girlfriend,'

> We bail out
> Then take the jail back
> Niggas ('s) united
> Our first date, couldn't wait to see you naked
> Touch you in every secret place, I could hardly wait to bust freely
> Got you red-hot you so happy to see me.

We argue that the 'bailing out' that precedes 'taking the jail back' is fundamentally connected to the shatkarma business of touching 'her,' i.e. 'his gun,' in 'every secret place' as a prerequisite to 'busting freely.'

Within a similar logic, in 'Let Them Thangs Go,' off *R U Still Down? (Remember Me)*, Tupac says,

> I'm quick to split the shit and get ya open
> Straight outta Oakland
> Fuck the law, get ya jaw broken
> Ba ba ba bang bang, nigga, it's a stick up D
> Turn the kick up I'm ready to rip the shit up, G.

This idea of 'splitting the shit' or dividing the body between left and right, as well as front and back, in order to get one 'open,' from our position, can signify shatkarma or the art of letting 'them thangs go.' More still, from the album *Me Against the World*, in response to the haunting voices and rumors from his 'homies' that try and control his decisions in 'Temptations,' Tupac says (with the deep passionate voice that only Tupac could deliver), 'Give 'em the finger' and 'Everybody knows I'm ballin'/ Hand to God, gotta keep myself from fallin'.' Like the Buddha's 'earth touching gesture' that not only indicates his victory over the demon Mara and Mara's temptress daughters but also wards off and prevents future attacks from Mara, we argue that Tupac's 'finger' or his 'hand to God' that prevents him from 'fallin'' is both a shatkarma mudra and an implicit means to shatkarma catharsis.

In hatha yoga's order of operations, shatkarma precedes the bandhas, which are the most foundational of liberating techniques designed to raise the vital Kundalini energy from the base of the spine to the crown of the head as well as from the back of the body to the front. In *Moola bandha: The Master Key*, 19th-century Hindu monk and philosopher (greatly responsible for introducing the Western world to Hinduism) Swami Vivekananda describes the bandhas thusly:

> The word bandha...may be defined in several ways. A Sanskrit dictionary definition runs as follows: 'binding, tying a bond, tie, chain, fetter, a ligature, to catch, hold captive, arrest, imprison, fix, fasten, hold back, restrain, stop shut, close, to redirect, check, obstruct, clot and lock.' Bandha may also be defined analogously and is linked to the 'damming of a river,' 'building a bridge' or 'building over the sea.' This can be interpreted as meaning that a bandha is a vehicle to traverse the ocean of samsara, worldly existence, and to reach the other shore of enlightenment... Seen physically, moola bandha is the conscious, willful contraction of the perineum or cervix, uddiyana bandha of the solar plexus and Jalandhar a bandha of the throat... In most modern yogic literature, bandha is defined simply as a 'lock.' However, the true meaning of bandha is essentially paradoxical, for it is said that by locking or contracting certain muscles on the physical level a subtle process of 'unlocking' goes simultaneously on mental and pranic levels.

The bandhas, which we understand to account for at least one modality of Jung's canalization of entropic libidinal energy, begins at the 'floor' or bottom of the body and works the libidinal energy upward along the spine through the stomach and the throat until the buildup of redirected pressure 'unlocks' divine, mental power. This, we argue, is what Tupac refers to as 'taking the jail *back*' (our italics) in 'Me and My Girlfriend' and as a 'stick up' in 'Let Them Thangs Go.'

Where Swami Vivekananda provides further clarification for what Jung calls the canalization of entropic libidinal energy with his definition of the yogic bandhas and does so by describing the bandhas through technological analogies to locks, dams, and bridges, the notion of a proper psychic mechanism being introduced for the achievement of enlightenment is an advanced technique that, like the shatkarmas, is implied and alluded to only through encrypted tropology. We turn our attention again to Svatmarama's *Hatha Yoga Pradipika* for a mythic and anecdotal example, which we will use as a model to analyze psychic mechanisms in Tupac:

> In the *Bhagavat Purana,* one of the richest of the ancient texts of Indian mythology and symbolism, we find a legend which is more than merely a legend. In a battle with the demons the gods were losing: they had considered themselves divinely superior to the forces of the world (the demoniac), but these forces stood more safely and firmly upon their ground. Brahma, whom the gods implored for help, ascended with the threatened ones to the Lord of the World, Vishnu, to ask his advice.
> 'Make peace with the demons,' he urged them, 'and churn with their help the nectar of immortality. The divine alone is as powerless as the earthly alone. Together you should churn the ocean of milk until it turns into the nectar of immortality.'
> So together the sworn enemies took the mountain Mandara, the backbone of the universe, wound around it the serpent Vasuki in three-and-one-half turns, and alternately pulling on the head (the demons) and the tail (the gods), they began to churn the terrestrial ocean of milk.
> But soon the mountain became too heavy for the diligent ones, and slowly it sank lower and lower. Then Vishnu transformed himself into a tortoise, dove to the bottom of the ocean, and raised the mountain so that the work could be completed.

In the notorious mythic anecdote that Svatmarama takes from the *Bhagavat Purana*, the only way for the gods to subdue the demons is, like Jesus at the wedding in Cana, to alchemically 'churn the ocean of milk until it turns into the nectar of immortality.' This occurs at the 'mountain' referred to as 'the backbone of the universe.' When the mountain threatens to fall, not only does Vishnu activate a bandha-like bind to support the mountain so the 'work' can be 'completed,' but he transforms himself into a 'tortoise,' an object, tool, or, in Jungian terms, a mechanism to canalize the entropic libidinal energy at the 'mountain's floor' to transfer energy to its 'summit.'

In 'Me and My Girlfriend,' similar yet distinct from the *Bhagavat Purana*, Tupac alludes to what Jung calls psychic mechanisms for canalization not in the figure of a tortoise but in that of a gun. Like the tortoise in the *Bhagavat Purana* whose job it is to hold up 'the backbone of the universe' and direct energy from low to high, Tupac's 'girlfriend/ gun,' additionally referred to as a 'messiah,' not only attacks 'demons' in Tupac's head; Tupac's 'girlfriend/ gun' attacks history itself: 'Love to watch you at a block party, beggin for drama/ While unleashing on the old-timers, that's on my mama.' A mechanism for cleansing out the old to keep current with the present moment, Tupac's speaker's 'girlfriend/ gun' does violence against even his mother, thereby effectively erasing his own point of origin and landing him in an alternate state of (non)existence.

That Tupac's 'girlfriend/ gun' is an object, tool, or mechanism that his speaker can join with and disconnect from is referenced in various ways in 'Me and My Girlfriend.' Here is one example:

> Talking loud when I tell you be quiet
> You move the crowd, busting rounds, activating a riot
> That's why I love you so, no control, down to roll, unleash
> After a hit you break apart then back to one piece.

This stage of not linking but now disconnecting parallels the famous lesson the Buddha teaches in his raft parable from the *Alagaddupama Sutta*. Here, instead of a tortoise holding up a mountain or a gun that exorcizes demons, we are presented with a raft that allows its rider to pass from one shore to another. The Buddha's message in his raft parable is that the purpose of the raft is for 'crossing over,' not 'holding onto,' and that once a monk uses a 'raft' it is no longer necessary and should be discarded.

The business of letting go of the past, or the desire for repetition – the act of transforming today and tomorrow into another programmatic version of yesterday – is what the shatkarmas, the bandhas, and the psychic mechanisms fashioned for advanced redirection of kundalini energy are about. In essence, they, and all of yoga, are methods for practicing the art of dying so that vital life, not a frozen and *a priori* existence, can emerge, which is why in 'Holla At Me,' off *All Eyes On Me*, Tupac says:

> I let the world know, nigga, you a coward
> You could never be live until you die
> See the motherfuckin' bitch in your eye.

Similar to Christ, who in *John* 3:1 states that 'Except a man be born again, he cannot see the kingdom of God,' Tupac says that one has to 'die' in order to 'live.' To be clear, it's implied that it isn't that the entire man has to die in either Christ or Tupac, but that part of him has to be done away with so that another part can be born. Troping on the figure of the gun as a symbol for a psychic mechanism again in 'This Ain't Livin',' off the posthumous *Until the End of Time*, Tupac says:

> This ain't livin'
> We givin' you jewels
> Use 'em as tools
> Explode on the industry and fade them fools
> …This for all of y'all that keep on raisin' hell
> Put a pistol in your hand and let you fade yourself
> It ain't right, what you put your mamma through, young G
> Gotta change your life, take the game from me.

Speaking to young people who are, to quote Tupac from 'Life of an Outlaw,' off *The Don Killuminati*, 'stuck in positions' where they are living out stereotypical 'dead' lives and effectively participating in their own oppression, Tupac tells them he's giving them 'tools' to be used to 'fade themselves.'

The final motif in Tupac we want to highlight in this chapter is the figure of psychic mechanisms in Tupac as modalities of violent communication. Following are a series of quotes from Tupac that combine figurations of tech with those referring to communication. In 'Me and My Girlfriend,' already quoted, Tupac's speaker says of his 'girlfriend/ gun,' 'Talking loud when I tell you be quiet/ You move the crowd, busting rounds, activating a riot.' From *All Eyez On Me*, in the track 'Got My Mind Made Up,' Tupac says:

> So mandatory my elevation
> My lyrics like orientation
> So you can be more familiar with the nigga you facin'

> We must be based on nothing better than communication
> Known to damage and highly flammable like gas stations.

In 'Life of an Outlaw,' off *Makaveli*, Tupac says:

> Make the track burst whenever I rap
> Attack
> Words bein' thrown to explode on contact.

For Tupac, as stated in 'Got My Mind Made Up,' humanity is 'based on… communication,' and communication is always political.

It is our understanding that this business of being 'based on… communication' is more than simply a Derridean observation. In contemporary literary theory, the French philosopher Jacques Derrida famously states that 'there is nothing outside of the text' in his chapter on Rousseau in *Of Grammatology*. There is a debate regarding what Derrida actually meant by this phrase, but it is frequently interpreted as a critique of semiologist Ferdinand de Saussure's concept of the referent. For Saussure, a sign consists of a signifier (a sound-image like a word), a signified (the mental concept the signifier produces in the subject), and the referent (the thing or object in the world being referenced). Therefore, words are arbitrary and have meaning(s) only because of the complex networks of contexts and relationships within which they are organized. By saying 'there is nothing outside of the text,' Derrida is typically understood to say that referents or real objects in the world never exist in and of themselves because they can only be accessed via signifying chains or through the words and images humans utilize to perceive them.

We could understand Tupac's lyrics 'We must be based on nothing better than communication' to make sense in a way similar to Derrida's logic. Still, in light of all the work we've unearthed concerning Tupac's preoccupation with psychic mechanisms – which, despite what Jung termed them, are very much material technologies and physical processes of canalization – we suggest otherwise. We propose that 'communication' is a much more profound series of material phenomena than Derrida considered, and that Tupac's philosophy of communication is grounded in his practice of the canalization of entropic libidinal energy designed to dislodge egocentrism. A physical material practice. A bodily practice. For Tupac, the evolutionary history that is 'deeper than the drive of mankind' is a modality of communication that not only connects humans to other humans but connects humans to all other life forms on the planet. Geological processes. Star formations. Photosynthesis. The conversion of DNA sequences. In utero development. Death. Rebirth. We argue they're all communication to Tupac. What Jung terms the individuation process not only opens one up to their realization that 'we must be based on nothing better than communication,' but, for Tupac, it equips them with psychic mechanisms capable of being utilized as thug-life weapons of political warfare to be used to bring others to this realization, controversially, whether they're ready to accept this reality or not.

It's not just that Tupac marks his diction and rhymes as 'words' that are 'thrown to explode on contact.' He figures his psychic mechanisms themselves as types of 'words' that are themselves able to communicate this reality through body language writ large – body language in how they afford connections and pathways internally that otherwise wouldn't be accessible and body language that relies on others to signify and also signifies something 'troublesome' to others: a 'death' that they have to face in order to 'live.'

Possibly more so than others, the Hindus exemplify this notion of the psychic mechanism as a form of language through the lingam symbol.

Encyclopedia Britannica defines the lingam thusly:

> [It is] a votary object that symbolizes the god Shiva and is revered as an emblem of generative power. The lingam appears in Shaivite temples and in private shrines throughout India… It is a smooth cylindrical mass. Often it rests in the center of a lipped, disk-shaped object, the yoni, which is an emblem of the goddess Shakti. Ancient Sanskrit texts such as the *Mahabharata* and the Puranas relate narratives that identify the lingam as the phallus of Shiva.

Wendy Doniger thoroughly analyzes the transition in *Encyclopedia Britannica* from signifying the lingam exclusively as a phallic symbol to its now more complex syntax that accounts for the lingam not solely as a symbol of the phallus but as a more abstract sign for creative potential more broadly. In her work "God's Body, or, the Lingam Made Flesh,"

Doniger's sweeping analysis concludes that, like many mythic symbols, their meanings not only change over time but they mean different things to different people: '[M]any Hindus have regarded the *lingam* as both abstract, without (sexual) qualities, and particular, with (sexual) qualities.' We argue two things about the lingam as it pertains to our analysis of psychic mechanisms for the canalization of entropic libidinal energy in Tupac: (1) we follow Joseph Campbell in suggesting that most religious symbols externally represent internal potentiality or capabilities between the internal and the external relative to the individuation process, and (2) French psychoanalyst Jacques Lacan's work about the phallus has the power to shut down the whole debate as to whether the lingam is a phallic symbol or not, because, for Lacan, the phallus is a consistently misunderstood object/ phenomenon.

In his dizzying analysis of not only the role of the phallus in Freud but also the phallus as a symbol in ancient times, Lacan states the following in "The Signification of the Phallus":

> The phallus can be better understood on the basis of its function... In Freudian doctrine, the phallus is not a fantasy... Nor is it as such an object (part-, internal, good, bad, etc.) inasmuch as 'object' tends to gauge the reality involved in a relationship. Still less is it the organ – penis or clitoris – that it symbolizes... For the phallus is a signifier, a signifier whose function, in the intrasubjective economy of analysis, may lift the veil from the function it served in the mysteries. For it is the signifier that is destined to designate meaning effects as a whole, insofar as the signifier conditions them by its presence as signifier.

We understand Lacan to state here that the phallus is a dynamic object or what Jung would call a psychic mechanism for canalizing entropic libidinal energy. It is none of the possible objects of desire but is rather a motor for desire itself. The phallus is, in short, a process of production that underpins any signified or referent, be they penis, clitoris, desired other, nonsexual sublimation, or otherwise. It relies on and transforms energy throughout a set of relations.

In Lacan's language, the phallus is a word or signifier that not only draws energy from its milieu but that also produces an impact or signified both in the subject and in the subject's environment. With this understanding, we can look more closely at Tupac's highly alliterative track 'If I Die Tonight' off *Me Against the World*. The track begins with Tupac paraphrasing Shakespeare's *Julius Caesar*: 'A coward dies a thousand deaths/ A soldier dies but once.' Then Tupac says, 'They say pussy and paper is poetry power and pistols/ Plotting on murdering motherfuckers before they get you.' These lines exemplify Tupac's understanding of his use of psychic mechanisms as a means of linguistic, political warfare, referencing the war of self against egomania and the fight against the egomania in others that takes place through body language, vocalizations, and writing simultaneously. Like the Hindu lingam combined with the yoni, Tupac's words reference a psychic mechanism that is neither masculine nor feminine exclusively but is indicative of their combined generative capabilities as they draw energy from their environments and metamorphosize them. For Tupac, 'pussy and paper' (the active feminine or the yoni when linked with the lingam) not only houses but also generates 'poetry power and pistols (the passive masculine or the active body made active by way of its submission to passivity).' These lines describe a mechanic attack against the egocentrism within that precedes any attack against the ego without: 'Plotting on murdering motherfuckers before they get you.' Even the term 'motherfuckers' here has to be reconsidered when one recognizes that the yoni in Hinduism is both marked as the mother's womb and is located within all human beings, not just literal women. For Tupac, not only are psychic mechanisms the preparations one takes to diffuse one's own spiritual poverty, they are the tools one adopts to go to war against poverty in the world. Tools for sex, for writing, for action, tools that can be utilized however one wants.

Lingam and Yoni, Cambodian, Norton Simon Museum, Pasadena, CA

Chapter 3

Tupac and the Ecstasy of God

'It's time for us as a people to start makin' some changes. Let's change the way we eat. Let's change the way we live. And let's change the way we treat each other. You see, the old way wasn't working so it's on us to do what we gotta do, to survive.'

Tupac Shakur, from 'Changes'

In "Unfortunate Son: The Roots of Tupac Shakur's Rebellion," journalist Travis Kitchens argues that Tupac was highly interested in literature that describes how near-death experiences can operate as doorways to the sacred:

> Along with classics by Toni Morrison and James Baldwin, Tupac's personal library was filled with works of mysticism and philosophy. He read Timothy Leary's acid classic *The Psychedelic Experience,* Catholic mystic Thomas Merton's *No Man Is an Island* and *Dark Night of the Soul,* a mystical text from the 16th century illuminating the process of spiritual evolution and rebirth. Tupac's first manager, Leila Steinberg, has said that Tupac was fascinated by Aldous Huxley and psychedelic drugs, which largely deal with the idea of spiritual regeneration through near-death experiences and contemplation.

The theory that one can come close to death as an act of numinous regeneration is an old idea with many reiterations and variations.

Philosopher Georges Bataille espouses this idea with a style and sensibility uncannily similar to Tupac's. Even though we have no evidence of Tupac reading Bataille, their interests are so entangled that we feel that Bataille is the most appropriate lens to begin scrutinizing Tupac's thoughts and lyrics about the experience of divine rapture.

Georges Bataille was a controversial French intellectual who took immense inspiration from German philosopher Friedrich Nietzsche, whom we know Tupac also read. Bataille's writing spanned various genres – literature, philosophy, sociology, and economics – but he is probably best known for his interests in eroticism, death, and human sacrifice. Bataille and others formed a secret society called Acephale, whose famous symbol is the image of a beheaded man whose genitalia has been castrated and skulled.

In our minds, the Acephale image comes very close to Hindu images of the goddess Kali, not just because they both feature decapitated men but, more importantly, because they both use the figure of decapitation to indicate the liberation that follows the collapse of egocentrism. Apparently, Bataille took the notion of decapitation to severe heights; as legend has it, he and other Acephale members made it publicly known that they would willingly subject themselves to beheading if anyone could garner the nerve to do the deed. No one responded.

We suggest that Bataille's work *The Accursed Share* not only sutures together some of his most important ideas but that his notions of general economy and sacrifice laid bare therein are extremely useful tools for beginning to make sense of Tupac's philosophy of sacred ecstasy. In *The Accursed Share*, any entity, be it an organism like a human body or a structured social form like a nation-state, has particular economic interests. Bataille called these particular economic interests 'restricted economy.' Every restricted entity, however, reaches an excessive limit where it confronts the paradox of both not having enough energy to continue expanding and having more than enough for its own sustenance. At these moments, the 'general economy' of which the restricted is a part becomes glaringly apparent. 'General economy' is the expansive totality of which the restricted is only a fragment, and, with changing perspectives relative to scale, this game of finding the general in relation to the restrictive is a forever widening or shrinking game of fractals (the human heart is restrictive until one recognizes that it's part of a general body, yet the body is restrictive until one sees it as part of the planet, but the planet is restrictive seen from the vantage of the solar system, and so on).

For Bataille, when any restrictive entity reaches that paradoxical moment where it has more than it needs to sustain itself and not enough to expand, it is confronted with a critical choice: further expansion that can only be accomplished by violently taking the additional excess it needs to increase or by wasteful expenditure. The former, for Bataille, always contradictorily backfires against the restricted entity and also brings unnecessary harm to others, while the latter offers the restricted entity a joyous encounter and connection with the larger general economy at the same time that it spreads energy and wealth abroad in a sporadic celebration of diversity and life affirmation. To provide some clarity concerning Bataille's terminology, wasteful expenditure is 'wasteful' because it is the antithesis of expansion. Waste, in other words, carries a positive value for Bataille.

> The least burdensome form of life is that of a green micro-organism (absorbing the sun's energy through the action of chlorophyll), but generally vegetation is less burdensome than animal life. Vegetation quickly occupies the available space. Animals make it a field of slaughter and extend its possibilities in this way; they themselves develop more slowly. In this respect, the wild beast is at the summit: its continual depredations of depredators represent an immense squandering of energy. William Blake asked the tiger: 'In what distant deeps or skies burned the fire of thine eyes?' What struck him in this way was the cruel pressure, at the limits of possibility, the tiger's immense power of consumption of life. In the general effervescence of life, the tiger is a point of extreme incandescence. And this incandescence did in fact burn first in the remote depths of the sky, in the sun's consumption.

Even when it isn't apparent, decapitation is always on Bataille's mind. Here, we see it in Bataille's reading of Blake's poem when the sunlight ironically emerges in the tiger's eyes, almost as though at that moment of elliptical return, the tiger is figuratively decapitated in his realization that the food chain is non-hierarchical. In occupying his position at the top, he has managed to transcend absolutely nothing. He isn't above the sun that feeds the plants, which, in turn, feeds the animals. Even at the top of the food chain, the tiger is still at the sun's mercy.

Bataille, in a change of scale, locates a kind of sublime decapitation not only in food chains but also in the strange connection that unites humanity's subterranean thoughts about death and sex:

> In reality, when we curse death we only fear ourselves... We lie to ourselves when we dream of escaping the movement of luxurious exuberance of which we are only the most intense form... In this respect, the luxury of death is regarded by us in the same way as that of sexuality, first as negation of ourselves, then – in a sudden reversal – as the profound truth of that movement of which life is the manifestation.

There is a strange mobius-strip-like loop that ties death to sex for Bataille. Certainly, he sees orgasm as an excessive moment of micro-death – a little decapitation – because, in one sense of the words, he marks it as a 'negation of self' or that moment where you lose yourself. The other sense of the phrase just expresses the reality that there is something undeniably mysterious (as well as beautiful) about the fact that when two people conceive a child, that child's development coincides with the aging and eventual deaths of the couple. This is the 'sudden reversal' for Bataille. It's when this both psychic and physical negation of self also turns into 'the manifestation of life' or birth. So it's in this way that we can go back and reread the beginning of the above quote when he states that 'when we curse death we only fear ourselves' because, for Bataille, the micro-death moment that is the excessive over-pouring of our parents' orgasms is the condition upon which we come into existence, and our development runs parallel to their decline. Therefore, we are death, so the fear of death is an act of self-alienation no less than the tiger telling himself he's superior to plants and sunlight.

There is a dual way in which Bataille studies sacrifice in *The Accursed Share*: sacrifice as an act of consumption and enterprise. With the example of the Aztecs, Bataille focuses on sacrifice as an act of consumption, which he views positively and associates with general economy. For the Aztecs, according to Bataille,

> The sun himself was in their eyes the expression of sacrifice. He was a god resembling man. He had become the sun by hurling himself into the flames of a brazier.

For Bataille, the god who throws himself into a fire to become the sun is effectively an enlightened tiger who says, 'I know I'm inextricably dependent upon and connected to plants and sunlight.' A man-like god, at reaching that paradoxical limit of personal excess and expansive scarcity, identifies with the perspective not of restrictive but of general economy and so chooses to affirm the diversity of life in an act of joyous consumption or waste. Bataille explores the antithetical sacrifice by analyzing Mexican military society based not on consumption or joyous distributions of excess but in productive enterprise or the expansion of a restrictive economy. Here, instead of sacrificing himself, the king sacrifices slaves he's captured in war:

> There is no possibility of a mistake here: This was a sacrifice of substitution. A softening of the ritual had occurred, shifting onto others the internal violence that is the moral principle of consumption. To be sure, the movement of violence that animated Aztec society was never turned more within than without… The substituting of a prisoner for the king was an obvious, if inconsequent, abatement of this sacrificial frenzy.

Rather than admit to having reached his limit and his dependency on the planet that sustains him, the enterprising king postpones his sacrifice and offloads it onto others to keep his rank and society expanding.

Tupac, we argue, espouses what Bataille terms consumption in his lyrics and identifies not with himself as a restrictive entity but as a general expression of that grand economy he terms 'God.' Yet, in a figurative twist on what Bataille calls enterprise, Tupac's thug pedagogy also advocates for the ritual sacrifice of others (an idea we began to explore in our introduction that considered Tupac as a specific kind of bodhisattva, a thug bodhisattva, and one we will expand upon here).

There's no better place to further explore the simultaneous celebration of wasteful consumption and the violent imposition of it onto others than in 'Intro/ Bomb First (My Second Reply)' off *Makaveli*. Consistently in this track, there is tension followed by release, accumulation followed by dissemination.

> Money-makin plans, pistol close at hand, swollen pockets
> Let me introduce the topic, then we drop it...
> Get me high, let me see the sun rise and fall.

Topics are brought up and then scattered. Height is followed by descent. But, in this very aggressive track, there are three aspects to Tupac's celebratory destruction: He shows that he celebrates accumulation and wasteful consumption (which we've already established), brags that his team does so, and attacks others with this principle. Speaking on Tupac's team, the Outlawz – who, in our minds, were not only his group of friends and fellow rapper-collaborators but also his effective graduate students – they, like bodhisattvas, are simultaneously committed to die for 'Tupac' and for those unenlightened others to whom they are directing their attack. And let's reiterate here, Tupac himself – the thing his students are 'down to die for' – is not a person as much as he is a placeholder for the sacred dissemination and redistribution of excess.

Speaking about the Outlawz in 'Intro/ Bomb First (My Second Reply),' Tupac says:

> My Outlaw niggas down to die for me (Know what I mean?)... This for my dogs down to die for y'all... My whole team trained to explode, ride or die.

So, like Bataille's Aztec god who threw himself into the fire to become the sun, Tupac positions himself as a model of consumptive life and then establishes that he isn't alone in his endeavors but is backed up by a whole team, his students the Outlawz as well as any listener who commits to the 'outlaw path.' They have been 'trained to explode,' which we interpret as the antithesis of enterprising accumulation. Moreover, it isn't only that Tupac and his students practice the art of self-detonation; they impose it on others, which is how Tupac twists Bataille's notion of enterprising sacrifice. It's with the establishment of this self-exploding practice that Tupac makes it clear that he and his students are out to sacrifice others in 'Intro/ Bomb First (My Second Reply).'

> Allow me to introduce first Makaveli the Don
> Hysterical, spiritual lyrics like *The Holy Qur'an*...
> Expose snakes cause they breed freely (see me ride)
> Located worldwide like the art of graffiti...
> In every city you'll find me
> Look for trouble right behind me...
> Niggas ducking from my guillotine stare
> I'm right there, my every word a fuckin nightmare...
> Extreme venom, no mercy when we all up in 'em
> Cut 'em down, to hell is where we send 'em...
> Murder motherfuckers lyrically, and I'm not gonna cry

What seems strikingly clear in this series of excerpts from 'Intro/ Bomb First (My Second Reply)' is not only that Tupac's attacks are lyrical, symbolic, or psychic but that the thing he identifies with here or the speaker of this track identifies with is something common: 'Hysterical, spiritual lyrics... Located worldwide like the art of graffiti... In every city you'll find me... My every word a fuckin nightmare... Murder motherfuckers lyrically.' Although the global phenomenon Tupac links himself to here comes about through oral transmission, Tupac's promise to deliver the experience of hysteria, trouble, nightmares, and hell, all the while, seems to be a very real promise.

We argue that the business of verbally bringing hell to others is a means of teaching enlightenment for Tupac, and nothing in 'Intro/ Bomb First (My Second Reply)' highlights this more than the fact that at the end of the song, following his verbal attack, Tupac says, 'Let us pray, my niggas, for we definitely have sinned.' Tupac was conflicted about the ethics of his pedagogy, but all the same, he found it necessary. We get this attitude at various places throughout Tupac's work. The track 'This Ain't Livin' off *Until the End of Time* underscores it clearly when Tupac says:

> Let's go see what our enemies talkin' about
> When G's enter the house nobody's walkin' out
> This ain't livin. It's similar to prison. We trapped.

For the chorus, an R & B singer says, 'Can't find a better way to break through.' Then Tupac says:

> This ain't livin I gotta do what I gotta do… We givin' you jewels
> Use 'em as tools
> Explode on the industry and fade them fools.

In 'This Ain't Livin' Tupac promises his listeners 'jewels' that can be used as 'tools' to 'explode' the 'industry' (which we already analyzed from one perspective in the chapter dealing with Tupac's sacred biotech); but he also – and this is what we want to highlight here – with frustration, admits that his method is going to take his listeners to their 'enemies' and deliver them to something 'like prison' and that this way isn't 'livin' but that he's resolved to this method not because it's fun or optimal but because he 'can't find a better way.'

There are several approaches to framing Tupac's problematic pedagogy within a larger context of ideas. Perry Miller's work 'Jonathan Edwards,' highlighting the famous American preacher's belief that he could craft an oration style that re-created the experience of hell for his congregation to bring about mass conversions and how it helped lead up to the Great Awakening, certainly comes to mind. However, we feel it's best to turn once again – now in more detail – to a work we know Tupac read, St. John of the Cross' *Dark Night of the Soul*. Of Spanish descent, St. John of the Cross was a controversial Carmelite reformist who was jailed for his beliefs before escaping prison. He died of erysipelas in 1591, and his works were published in 1618. St. John's text effectively describes the hellish experience a practitioner undergoes as they labor to unite their soul (depicted as a feminine bride) with God (represented as a masculine bridegroom) in what is figured as a sacred marriage in the tradition of *Song of Songs* from the *Bible* as well as the writings of St. Paul and many other Christian mystics.

In *Dark Night of the Soul*, St. John marks over and over again that the hellish dangers incurred along the 'road' that is the 'dark night of the soul' are specifically dangers invited by what he terms 'beginners,' that these dangers arise through the beginners' amateur spiritual exercises, and that the upshot of the 'dark night of the soul' is to lead beginners to God so that God can instruct them in better practices:

> Since, then, the conduct of these beginners upon the way of God is

ignoble, and has much to do with their love of self and their own inclinations, as has been explained above, God desires to lead them farther. He seeks to bring them out of that ignoble kind of love to a higher degree of love for Him, to free them from the ignoble exercises of sense and meditation (wherewith, as we have said, they go seeking God so unworthily and in so many ways that are unbefitting), and to lead them to a kind of spiritual exercise wherein they can commune with Him more abundantly and are free more completely from imperfections.

St. John is never explicit about the nature of the 'ignoble kind of love' that constitutes the spiritual exercises of a beginner. Still, he states overtly that they involve sense and meditation, and it's heavily implied that these amateur forms of prayer – which he calls 'impure acts and motions' – are of a sexual nature:

[T]hey [beginners] have many imperfections which might be described as spiritual luxury... For it often comes to pass that, in their very spiritual exercises, when they are powerless to prevent it, there arise and assert themselves in the sensual part of the soul impure acts and motions, and sometimes this happens even when the spirit is deep in prayer.

Even the devil, posing as a spirit guide, is said to come to the beginner in these amateur meditations or 'impure acts and motions' and 'succeeds in portraying to them very vividly things that are most foul and impure.' But this hellish experience, all the same, is an experience 'wherein the soul is strengthened and confirmed in the virtues, and made ready for the inestimable delights of the love of God.' In short, the dark night of the soul is an experience of hell that burns the fat of one's soul, leading one to God and advanced spiritual practices.

Where it's clear that St. John of the Cross states that the 'ignoble exercises of sense and meditation' start one out on the road leading through the purgation of hell to a marriage of one's soul with God, he's very cautious about outlining these exercises in any detail, and, although they are implicitly necessary steppingstones along the way, he doesn't place any positive value on them. He just leaves it up to the reader to infer their purpose and place in the whole scheme of what Jung would term the individuation process. The opposite position, however, is taken up in the transgressive tradition of Vajrayana Buddhism, which we have reason to believe Tupac was aware of, either through Jack Kornfield –

whom he read – through something he picked up from Leila Steinberg, or from elsewhere in his vast City of Angels.

Vajrayana Buddhism is known as the 'thunderbolt vehicle' and claims to be the fastest path to enlightenment. That said, like *Dark Night of the Soul*, it vehemently cautions practitioners in many ways against the dangers of this path and adheres to a very hierarchical structure, including rigorous teacher-student relationships, to help practitioners navigate enlightenment's labyrinth of hazards. In the Vajrayana tradition, a student must get permission from a master before studying and practicing specific techniques. Chogyam Trungpa Rinpoche, the Tibetan monk who escaped oppression from the Chinese government before coming to the West to teach Vajrayana very patiently and cautiously, sometimes focuses on what he calls 'spiritual materialism,' or the ego's ability to appropriate any spiritual practice, and 'crazy wisdom,' which, despite how it might sound, indeed emphasizes that Buddhism isn't about mystic magic but is rather about a commitment to deep sanity. He argues that spiritual enlightenment is the greatest achievement of humankind. Yet, simultaneously, he says that to set out on the path to enlightenment, one has to understand that one is 'about to become [an] egomaniac.' In *The Lion's Roar: An Introduction to Tantra*, Chogyam Trungpa is clear in stating that once one enters the path, there is no turning back, which can account for why Tupac so easily adapted this method to the figure of gang culture and gangsterism: 'Once you get onto this particular bandwagon, it is an ongoing journey without reverse and without brakes. You have no control over the horse that is pulling this carriage.' Chogyam Trungpa was very cautious about teaching Tantra and very outspoken in stating that, in America, it could cause more harm than good. Even though it is, in many ways, a transgressive path, like gang culture, it has many rules and laws that must be adhered to. Chogyam Trungpa compares interpreting the symbolism while on the Tantric path to the everyday laws of life in America:

> If you are speeding, you get a ticket. If you are driving too slow, you get a honk from behind. A red light means danger; a green light means go; an amber light means get ready to go or stop. If you try to cheat on your karmic debts, the tax authorities are going to get after you.

These are just some of the vague dangers Chogyam Trungpa cryptically warns students about. However, in his lectures, he never fails to go extremely slow and practices a deep withholding of technique when working with beginners.

Vajrayana, in our understanding, is for people who are already seriously beginning to suspect they've been unconsciously imprisoning themselves in encrusted, repressive skandha-structures, secretly building themselves invisible prisons of glass and then telling themselves they're really free. Vajrayana basically says, 'Okay. For you people who are ready, we're going to go ahead and let you see how you've been making yourself sick by showing you how to give yourself an extreme dose of the poison you've been slowly feeding yourself all along. We're going to get you to a place where you can put visible bars against your prisons of glass so you can see what you've unconsciously been doing.' It's not a method of making one sick and then giving one a cure so Vajrayana can say, 'Look. We made you better.' But there's always a danger of it becoming that, which is why a guru is supposed to determine which students actually need or are ready for transgressive methods. Once decided, it's the guru's job to be the student's anchor to 'Earth' while they go off and explore the depths of their own unconscious egomania or face their own shadow (in Jungian terms).

We argue that Tupac takes a complicated approach to this system. In one regard, we suggest that he widely distributes himself as the audio-visual teacher to masses of disenfranchised students – especially black students – because he believes that history has denied them the cultural and socioeconomic opportunities that would have allowed them to study the path to enlightenment. On being a teacher, Tupac, in a 1994 MTV interview, states:

> Every time I speak I want the truth to come out. Every time I speak I want a shiver… I'm not saying I'm gonna rule the world or I'm gonna change the world, but I guarantee you that I will spark the brain that will change the world.

Yet, in another sense, we suggest that, as an overtly political act, Tupac overthrows the kind of hierarchical, student-teacher system found in Vajrayana Buddhism altogether because he simply believes that there isn't enough time, and the stakes are too high. This, we argue, is a way of making sense of a neologism Tupac refers to frequently: 'killuminati,' which is basically a combination of 'kill' and 'illuminati,' the Illuminati being, for Tupac, a secret society of religious avant-garde who keep a monopoly on enlightenment practices and their powers. Additionally, the Illuminati signifies a specific configuration of one's own mechanism of internalized oppression, which is why Tupac not only attacks the Illuminati without but also attacks the Illuminati within. As he states in 'Hail Mary,' 'killuminati all through your body/ The blow's like a 12-gauge shotty.' Tupac, we argue, was a revolutionary who accepted all the baggage and high costs that come with any revolution. However, the dangers of his approach are comparable to someone who slips another a dose of LSD (or maybe PCP) to 'turn them on.' Ethically troublesome, to say the least. And, yet, all the while, his approach is deeply admirable because the people Tupac 'attacks' are those who are already susceptible to gangsterism, violence, and conquest. Those victimizers who, as once victims themselves, so deeply internalized the ideology of their oppressors that they now are unable to listen to reason. So we're likely talking about most hip-hop fans in general really. You know, Americans. And human beings across the planet. In other words, he attacks potential victimizers themselves in an effort to save them from doing something horrible. In an effort to protect them from themselves. But, at the same time, he attacks them to activate them as agents of radical change.

Speaking on Vajrayana Buddhism, its commitment to what some might call homeopathy, and its use of sexual practices, *Buddhist Thought: A Complete Introduction to the Indian Tradition* states:

> The notion that mental states ordinarily conceived of as negative could be employed as a means of effectively traversing the path to Buddhahood becomes a significant feature of the Vajrayana phase of tantric Buddhism. The *Hevajra Tantra* (II: ii, 51) declares that 'the world is bound by passion, also by passion it is released.' It gives a homeopathic argument by way of justification: 'One knowing the nature of poison may dispel poison with poison, by means of the very poison that a little of which would kill other beings' (op. cit: II: ii, 46). Of the passions, it is sexual craving and pleasure that tend to be placed in the foreground, sexual bliss being homologized with the great bliss of awakening.

In Vajrayana Buddhism, some texts even go so far as to retell the story of the Buddha's path to enlightenment to argue that Tantra's esoteric and transgressive methods were part of his transformation all along. This is precisely what we argue Tupac does in 'Toss It Up,' also off *Makaveli*. He takes the logic at play in St. John of the Cross that depicts a marriage between the soul and God and sexualizes it, or, rather, he highlights that it was always sexual to begin with.

'Toss It Up,' in some ways, is received as a diss track aimed at Tupac's once-collaborator Dr. Dre, not only because Dre is mentioned explicitly in the work but also because it samples 'No Diggity,' a song by the R & B group Backstreet that both features Dre rapping and uses his beat. However, based on our analysis of what we're calling Tupac's thug pedagogy, we have a different understanding of the diss that is laid down therein. With Tupac's pedagogy, he lyrically sacrifices or attacks others not to create a substitution wherein he can avoid being sacrificed and thus strengthen his enterprise. He brings people to hell because, for him, it's the fastest way to God, and, for some, it's the only path they're willing to hear, which isn't to say that Tupac doesn't also teach advanced methods that instruct practitioners in avoiding hell altogether. He does, and it's the focus of the chapter of this book dealing with Tupac's sacred biotech. But for those unwilling to hear and accept advanced techniques, Tupac is ready to send his students to hell in hopes that in that place they will find the humility and understanding requisite to receive a different set of instructions. So it is in this way that Tupac truly loves his enemies. Moreover, it's hard to classify 'Toss It Up' as a simple diss track because Tupac doesn't address Dre until the second verse. The first verse, in our interpretation, reiterates and reevaluates the motif of a marriage between the speaker and God similar to that found in St. John of the Cross, not to mention Hinduism, *Kabbalah*, Gnosticism, St. Paul, Vajrayana Buddhism, and other spiritual traditions that think in these terms. What's at odds between Tupac and St. John of the Cross is that, as in the Vajrayana tradition, Tupac explicitly figures this divine communion as sexual.

'Toss It Up' begins with what sounds like Tibetan monks chanting in the background. When Tupac starts to rap, he says:

> Lord have mercy, Father help us all
> Since you supplied your phone number, I can't help but call.

We believe it's safe to say that many people interpret these lines on a surface level, which is to say they understand the 'you' Tupac addresses to be a regular female. She has given Tupac her phone number, and now Tupac is praying to God to have mercy on him because his desire for her is so strong. Fine. There are many ways to interpret this song, and, while we wouldn't discredit any of them, we very much want to highlight that the piece can be read otherwise. First, we argue that a regular song about sex with a female doesn't have a good reason to include Tibetan monks chanting at the beginning of it. Second, we argue that 'Lord,' 'Father,' and the 'you' who has supplied Tupac with their 'phone number' can, within the esoteric traditions we've been exploring throughout this project, all be read as the same person: God. It's God who has given Tupac His phone number, and God is whom Tupac calls in the first verse of 'Toss It Up.'

To further corroborate this point, we mark that one of the hallmark techniques of Vajrayana Buddhism is a complex form of deity yoga that leads to a pinnacle where the practitioner simultaneously merges with the deity in sexual union, murders the deity, and replaces or becomes the deity or fully awakened Buddha. In Zen Buddhism, a famous koan attributed to Linji Yixuan also espouses the murderous aspect of this logic: 'If you meet the Buddha on the road, kill him.' This simultaneous act of violence, merger, and emergence, notwithstanding, is always internally manifested. The body is the primary point of contact for all Vajrayana methods. The *Hevajra Tantra* states: 'The School, we say, is the body. The monastery is the womb.' So it's by way of this understanding that, to put it clearly, we interpret the 'God' with whom Tupac engages in sacred intercourse to be just as much a veiled aspect of self as the anima and the unconscious in the Jungian system. *Kabbalah* (which we know Tupac studied), as well as other traditions, combine the anima aspect of self with the God aspect of self by figuring the female zone – Shekhinah, meaning 'dwelling' – as the Divine Consort of God so that 'she' becomes a portal through which God comes, goes, possesses oneself, impregnates oneself, and evolves one's soul.

This *Kabbalah* notion of the female aspect of self as the passive dwelling through which God enters and overlaps with oneself, we argue, provides clarification as to how and why Tupac so fluidly switches between referencing God as Father and then, in the next moment, as a female with whom he's having intercourse. Along this line of reasoning, after these opening two lines from 'Toss It Up,' the song takes an abrasive turn toward the overtly sexual.

> Lord have mercy, Father help us all
> Since you supplied yo' phone number, I can't help but call
> Time for action, conversation, we relaxin', kickin' back
> Got you curious for Thug Passion, now picture that
> Tongue kissin', hand full of hair, look in my eyes
> Time to make the bed rock, baby look how it rise
> Me and you movin in the nude, do it in the living room
> Sweatin' up the sheets, it's the thug in me.

Tupac, in these lyrics, can be understood to say that since God has provided His 'phone number,' which we read as a channel through which to communicate with Him, Tupac can't help but place that phone call, as though it's the realization of his deepest longing.

In a lecture on Tantric Buddhism, religious studies scholar Alan Watts, like Tupac, compares Kundalini awakening – the Hindu tradition that Watts and many others fold into Vajrayana or Tantric Buddhist practice as its predecessor – to calling God on the phone:

> [Y]ou arouse the sexual energy [in some tantric practices] but instead of dissipating it you send it up the spinal column into the brain. You all know, presumably, the symbolism of yoga, of the Kundalini, that at the base of the spine there is what's called the serpent – Kundalini, the serpent power – and that the object of yoga is to send your concentrated energy... up the spine, energizing each chakra center... [like a] nervous telephone exchange... Finally, he gets into the thousand-petaled lotus in the head, and everything is lit up. You know all things, and eventually he goes out the top of the head, the sun door... and you're liberated... '

First, here, we'll mark again (as we have in a previous chapter) that there is an ongoing motif in Tupac where he figures himself as driving a 'drop top' vehicle. This is even expressed in 'Toss It Up' when Tupac says, 'Late night, hit the highway, drop the top/ I pull over, gettin' busy in the parking lot.' We understand Tupac's 'drop top' to potentially reference what Watts calls 'the sun door' at the top of the head. According to the trajectory of Kundalini yoga and Tantric Buddhism, this is a gateway that is accessed through both horizontal and vertical energy redirection by way of the spine that Watts and Tupac both figure as a medium through which a figurative phone call to God can be made – a 'nervous telephone exchange.'

We can even see Tupac metaphorically alluding to this trajectory of energy redirection in 'Still I Rise' (his homage to Maya Angelou's famous poem) off the album with the same title:

> Somebody wake me, I'm dreamin'
> I started as a seed, the semen
> Swimmin' upstream, planted in the womb while screamin'
> On the top was my pops, my mama screamin' stop
> From a single drop, this is what they got
> Not to disrespect my peoples, but my papa was a loser
> Only plan he had for mama was to fuck her and abuse her
> Even as a little seed, I could see his plan for me
> Stranded on welfare, another broken family.

We first mark that Tupac begins this verse by stating that he's living in a dream he needs to be awakened or *enlightened* from. By personifying himself as semen, Tupac takes us into the body on a micro level, but the nature of and trajectory of this energy transference is ambiguous in a way that allows us to read it through a Tantric frame because Tupac states that, as 'seed,' he swims 'upstream,' which can be interpreted to denote literal verticality within oneself like Watts' 'nervous telephone exchange' up the spine. Tupac, here, can be understood to describe a sacred, or what Jung would term a Whole body with both male and female components. Like in Taoism, which we'll analyze further momentarily, the male, paternal authority associated with what Freud calls the ego ideal is positioned up top: 'On the top was my pops.' Contrarily, the female maternal principle is set at the bottom. Opposite Taoism, where the goal is to have the male aspect dominate and subjugate the female aspect, Tupac, similar to Tantra's body/ female positive position, states that the 'father's' plan is to 'fuck' and 'abuse' the mother, thereby making synonymous his imperative at the beginning of the song to 'wake up' and his latter directive to overthrow 'the father.' This upsurge of energy that attacks the father, schematically positioned as the head of the body, is again evocative of the kinds of sacred decapitations we've already looked at in both Hinduism's Kali and the concept of wasteful sacrifice in Bataille.

Alan Watts goes on to explain in his lecture on Tantra that there is some discrepancy between, in his terms, Buddhist approaches to sending sexual energy up the spine and Taoist methods, but, based on our research, we suggest that the debates surrounding these procedures exist within each tradition as much as between the two. Watts states, however, that Tantra instructs one to redirect one's libidinal energy without ever releasing it. In contrast, Taoism says that energy can be released following stimulation behind the genitals, thereby redirecting it. An excessive redirection of amorous energy – if we can just pause for a moment to be clear about the stakes in play – is the very thing Freud, in "On Narcissism," attributes to the development of that internal policing apparatus he terms the ego ideal (which we analyzed in a previous chapter, and compared to what in Buddhist terms would be perceived as a rigid or oppressive skandha formation). It's for this very reason that Vajrayana Buddhism repeatedly underscores the idea of homeopathy – poison used to defeat poison. The very thing Freud labels as the problem, according to Vajrayana Buddhists, is the solution to the problem if it is pushed to its extreme. Tupac, notwithstanding, follows a logic similar to that of Bataille regarding his position on this debate in 'Temptations,' off *Me Against the World*, a destination our analysis will detour into before returning to further read 'Toss It Up.'

'Temptations' is, without argument, a track about the conflict of fidelity. However, many readers may interpret the track to be about the struggle of a famous and sexually desirable person to remain monogamous. At the same time, in our reading, it's more about Tupac's commitment to his craft and the demands of capitalizing on it than his commitment to a partner. A personal relationship with another and the sexual intercourse accompanying it is the primary temptation confronting Tupac in the song. The partner he's drawn to cheat on in 'Temptations' is not a person, in other words, but is his work.

> I want the fame, but the industry's a lot like
> A crap game, ain't no time for commitment, I gotta go
> Can't be with you every minute Ms., another show
> And even though I'm known for my one night stand
> I wanna be an honest man.

Tupac struggles to be an honest man to his work because his work is sacred. Phrased differently, Tupac battles to be honest with God, and the real challenge of his conflict lies in the fact that the medium through which Tupac enacts his sacred pedagogy is the exhaustingly demanding music industry. Tupac wants 'the fame' because he seeks to reach as many students as possible, but to both ascertain and maintain creditable notoriety, he must labor tirelessly because the music business is unpredictable and demanding. Seen through a Tantric lens, the temptation for Tupac is the release of the libidinal energy he's employing both to make his own personal 'phone call' to God and, more basically, for his work in general. To elaborate briefly on the connection between sexual self-abandonment and work productivity, it's a frequently reiterated idea that 'sublimated' (or not-released/ redirected) sexual energy is seen as a kind of battery power that allows for increased work performance. This is one of the basic tenets of Freudianism that inspired both the Marxist Herbert Marcuse and the psychoanalyst Wilhelm Reich to see orgasm as revolutionary and anti-capitalist (if you're having intercourse in a capitalist system, you're not working, and, if you're not working, then you're not making your boss rich off your excess labor power – a kind of biopolitics). It was these thinkers who helped inspire the whole sexual liberation movement in America during the 1960s that Tupac's mother lived through and no doubt was, in some manner, influenced by (be it that she was a member of the Black Panthers, who were liberationists in their own right).

In 'Temptations,' orgasm itself is what threatens to offset both Tupac's spiritual 'honesty' and his infamously aggressive work ethic. The chorus to this track chants the voices of either guidance or temptation that haunt Tupac, saying, 'Give 'em the finger.' It is a complete aporia as to whether the chorus offers Tupac guidance or utters temptation because the object of predication is consistently ambiguous. Whether these voices are advising Tupac to say 'fuck off' to the industry, to say 'fuck off' to the sexual relationship, or rather to say 'fuck off' to both when appropriate at different points in time is indeterminate. What specifically interests us here, however, is the play between the pressurization of tension and its release, and Tupac, like Bataille, seems to value both in broad and polysemic ways:

> Can't hold it any longer, so let it go
> Open the gates to your waterfall up in heaven
> And don't worry, I let myself in, all I heard was
> Give 'em the finger.

Like Bataille, Tupac advocates for pressurized buildup followed by wasteful release. However, the fact that he references this release as a release that opens 'the gates' to a 'waterfall up in heaven' leaves the reader lingering once again in a zone of ambiguity. Certainly, in a conventional sense, orgasm can be and has been referred to figuratively as 'heaven.' Yet, at the same time, the 'phone call to God,' sometimes called Kundalini awakening or Tantric liberation, also explicitly thinks itself in terms of creating an altered state of consciousness that one could call 'heaven.' Furthermore, the advanced techniques of the shatkarms and the mudras that illuminate them, mentioned in a previous chapter – as well as the role 'giving the finger' plays in both actions – make it all the more difficult to know who or what the voices in the chorus encourage Tupac to reject. All of these disturbances that make it impossible to glean any single meaning from this track, if nothing else, deliver the message that it is critical to disrupt every routinization at the right time and with the right mindset and that diffusing any routine spawns new routines that are themselves in need of unsettling.

Linking back up with 'Toss It Up' and our exploration therein of what we argue is the phone call Tupac makes to God, the chorus of this track is of particular interest. Sung by a variety of R & B singers – Aaron Hall, Danny Boy, K-Ci, and JoJo – the hook, similar to Tupac's fluid oscillation that shifts between figuring God both as Father and as a female, espouses the male R & B singers saying some ambiguous phrases regarding gender that can easily be interpreted as marking themselves as female or feminine. We hear them sing, 'Female I like…,' which can be understood to say that the speaker is female-like, and 'Oh, it's K-Ci baby, mm that want you lady.' The last line ('that want you lady') can be read to qualify K-Ci, as though to say that he is that want-you-lady. He is the lady who desires. The chorus singers also chant puzzling phrases regarding the sexual exchange they describe. These multivalent statements make it sound as though they are just as likely referencing Kundalini/ Tantra as they are pointing to conventional intercourse, comments like 'baby you taste as fine as gravy' and 'Your body the kind I like-ah/ Big booty to the lung delight-ah.' Indeed, the phrase 'toss it up' itself can be understood to reference anal oral sex between two separate individuals. However, at the same time, especially after contemplating the pathway of Kundalini awakening described by Watts (and many others) – traveling from the bottom of the spine ('Big booty'), through the lungs ('to the lung delight-ah'), up to the top of the head – as well as Tupac's metaphor of a phone call made to God, 'toss it up' can also be interpreted as a figuration of sexual yoga or yoga methods figured sexually.

 This logic of forging a link with oneself in an act of sacred union (whether one is literally alone or with another, as, once one recognizes the anima, it's impossible to think of oneself as solitary again and, on a certain level, impossible to think of monogamy) allows us to read these lines in 'Toss It Up' as describing a 'sexual' exchange between Tupac and the God-aspect of himself that he refers to as the thug within, specifically in the lyric 'Sweatin' up the sheets, it's the Thug in me.' Here again, we don't doubt that many people interpret these lines as saying, 'It's the thug, gangster, or animal in me that drives me to approach my sex game with this female who gave me her number with so much passion.' However, like St. John of the Cross' *Dark Night of the Soul*, the Greek *hieros gamos*, or the Hindu affair of Radha and Krishna, 'Toss It Up' can also be read as a song about the 'marriage' between oneself and God. A marriage within. So these lines can be heard to say something more like, 'The Thug in me is the entity with which I wrestle in a generative intercourse that is always more than the sum of its parts.' In this light, it's as though Tupac takes a break from his dialogue with God – 'Me and you movin in the nude, do it in the living room' – to address himself (as though in an almost surprised moment of realization) and the listener to reveal to whom the 'you' refers: 'It's the thug in me.'

The idea of *God-within* being refigured as *Thug-within* makes much sense to us given a series of reasonings we see at play both in Tupac and in the kinds of logics that permeate Hindu and Vajrayana traditions (as well as others). As we argued in a previous chapter, a variety of stories tell of a group of Hindu Kali worshippers who called themselves 'thuggees' or 'thugs.' As legend has it, they duped English tourists and then sacrificed them to Kali. We've been arguing throughout this work as a whole and this chapter specifically that Tupac was also interested in offering his 'enemies' to Kali – which he would have spelled 'Cali' – by leading them to the hell that would awaken them. As is apparent in St. John of the Cross, once one is within the labyrinth of 'the dark night of the soul,' God delivers a new set of instructions that replace the inadequate methods of the beginner. By this reasoning, we argue that God can be interpreted as the original Thug. Meaning the idea of a program that takes one to and through hell can be interpreted as coming directly from God, and it's because of this reasoning that we can understand Tupac's lyric, 'Sweatin' up the sheets, it's the thug in me' from 'Toss It Up' to reference God. Tupac refers to God as the Thug within because, for Tupac, unlike St. John of the Cross, God isn't only the force that leads one through 'the dark night of the soul' – God is the gangster, thuggish force that brings one there in the first place. A closer analysis of this would reveal how highly controversial this position is because it would force readers to reconsider the clear distinctions that conventionally separate the goodness of God from evil or even God from the devil.

Even in the *Bible*, *Revelations* 16:15, God says, 'Behold, I come as a thief.' Along the lines of God being the Thug-within who takes away to provide and attacks to transform, there is an ongoing motif in Tupac where he addresses his 'nigga nature,' which he frequently exchanges with 'thug nature.' 'N.I.G.G.A,' Tupac makes clear in 'Words of Wisdom' from his first album *2Pacalypse Now*, is an acronym that means 'never ignorant getting goals accomplished.' On the track 'Niggaz Nature

Remix' from the posthumous *Until the End of Time*, Tupac attacks an unnamed 'female's' desire for illusion, fakeness, and dependency to introduce 'her' to 'nigga nature,' which we interpret as the antithesis of all her qualities. In the chorus, the R & B singer Lil' Mo sings,

> Kiss the girls, make 'em cry
> Thuggin life, and gettin high
> Why you gangsta all the time?
> That's a thug's nature,

and Tupac echoes, 'that's a nigga nature.' In *Luke* 14:26 from *The Bible*, Jesus says:

> If any man come to me, and hate not his father, and mother, and wife, and children, and brethren, and sisters, yea, and his own life also, he cannot be my disciple.

Jesus requires a complete commitment to impermanence and self-abandonment (to leave one's past, present, and future is to leave oneself) from his disciples, and it's in this vein that we understand 'nigga nature/ thug nature.' To clarify, we don't take this literally. Christianity requires one to hate 'themselves,' 'all they come from,' and 'all they produce' because 'oneself' has to 'die' in part to be 'born again' anew. In other words, the one who leaves to walk the path of enlightenment will not be the same one who arrives at their destination. To merge with 'God,' one cannot have any attachment to illusion or any dependency on others, including the self that one is at any given moment. Moreover, we argue that 'nigga nature/ thug nature' sounds a lot like 'Buddha nature.'

One of the most meaningful essays on the notion of 'Buddha nature' is written by professor of philosophy and religion Sallie B King. Her work on Buddha nature is significant because it rectifies some of the seeming contradictions of Buddhism surrounding the Buddhist notion of non-self:

> Buddhism, and especially early Buddhism, is known for the *anaiman* (no self) teaching... Zen Buddhism (Chinese Ch'an), in contrast, is known for its teaching that the single most important thing in life is to discover the 'true self.'

King, accepting as we have described in a previous chapter that in Buddhism there is no essential self but rather an ever-evolving collection of conditioned aggregates or skandhas, turns to the notion of Buddhist nature primarily found in the *Buddha Nature Treatise* to try and explain how the Zen tenet of self-discovery doesn't contradict the Buddhist principle of no self. In "The Buddha Nature: True Self as Action," King notes the following:

> Buddha nature is identified with the *tathagatagarbha*... As *garbha* may mean either womb or embryo, *tathagatagarbha* may stand for either womb of the Buddhas or embryonic Buddha. In other words, it can be seen either as the potential to realize enlightenment which we all possess or as perfect enlightenment itself.

According to the notion of Buddha nature, enlightenment is an embryo that is always present within oneself, but it is covered up by hardened skandha 'defilements' resulting from 'greed, anger, [and] ignorance.' King rectifies the seeming contradiction between the idea of non-self and self-discovery by essentially understanding Buddha nature as the realization that the true self is a non-self, an evolving self, or a self that practices not being but becoming: '[T]his lack of self is real; it *is* the real nature of things. Therefore it may be called a 'self.'' This true self as a core of non-attachment, a forever evolving and emptying becoming, is very possibly what Tupac references in 'Toss It Up' when he says, 'It's the thug in me' after informing listeners that he's made a 'sexualized' phone call to God, sex here, as in Buddhist Tantric practices, being almost unrecognizable as such – a repurposing of a basic function that completely alters the nature and quality of its being so much that it requires new terminology altogether. Jnanamudra and karmamudra are the terms Tantric Buddhists use to describe these meditative, sacred practices. For Vajrayana (which means the same thing as Tantric) Buddhists, this 'phone call to God' is very much not sex conventionally understood. It's something else entirely.

Now that we've established how the 'Thug in me' from 'Toss It Up' can refer to 'God within' or the embryonic, always-present but veiled-by-defilements aspect of Buddha nature, we return to 'Toss It Up' and its popular categorization as a diss track. Listeners can't access the second verse that addresses Dr. Dre without initially passing through the first verse, which we're interpreting as a verse describing a kind of sexual merging between Tupac and the simultaneously male and female God-aspect of himself within. A significant shift occurs, however, in the second verse. Whereas in the first verse, Tupac positions himself as the one who's undergoing the process of merging with or making a sacred phone call to the God-within, in the second verse, Tupac takes on the position of and acts as the mouthpiece for the God-within Dre and figures Dre as the one who's under attack from God's thuggish assault via a divine phone call or psychic possession. Where Tupac calls God in the first verse, God (figured by Tupac) calls Dre in the second:

> How do you want it? What's your phone number? I get around
> Cali Love to my true Thugs, picture me now
> Still down for that Death Row sound, searchin' for paydays
> No longer Dre Day, arrivederci
> Blown and forgotten, rotten for plottin' Child's Play
> Check your sexuality, as fruity as this Alize
> Quick to jump ship, punk trick, what a dumb move
> Cross Death Row, now who you gon' run to?
> Lookin' for suckers 'cause you similar
> Pretendin' to be hard, oh my God, check your temperature
> Screamin' Compton, but you can't return, you ain't heard
> Brothers pissed 'cause you switched and escaped to the burbs
> Mob on to this new era, 'cause we untouchable
> Still can't believe that you got 'Pac rushin you
> Up in you, bless the real, all the rest get killed
> Who can you trust, only time reveals, toss it up.

Here, Tupac does more in his first line than just list two songs from the *All Eyes On Me Album* ('How Do You Want It' and 'What'z Ya Phone #'), an album Dre helped produce, and follow them up with a reference to a previous track Dre had nothing to do with ('I Get Around') to suggest that Tupac can make hits with or without Dre's assistance. Tupac also establishes that he's taking on the position of God and entering Dre's psyche via a phone call. By asking Dre what his phone number is after already establishing in the first verse of 'Toss It Up' that phone calls in this track are tropological ciphers for conversations with

God, Tupac sets the stage and reveals to listeners that he's about to perform a sexualized inner dialogue between himself as God and Dre as a beginner on the path that is 'the dark night of the soul.'

Dre is marked as a beginner on the path to enlightenment when Tupac states, in more than just a reference to the famous horror movie, that Dre is 'rotten for plottin' Child's Play.' He is a 'child' in the game of enlightenment, 'rotten' with defilements and beginner practices, in the 'horror movie' of the shadow aspect of his own unconscious, which we have no shame in underscoring can very much be described as a series of ethical tests or temptations that one should very much aspire to pass by recourse to a strong sense of morality (to confront and move through the shadow realm does not mean one should succumb to it). This idea of Tupac as God simultaneously attacking and figuratively sexing Dre from within is further corroborated in this track toward the end of the second verse when Tupac, as God, says to Dre, 'Still can't believe that you got Pac rushin you/ Up in you, bless the real, all the rest get killed.' By no means do we interpret this line as a conventional diss. Here, Tupac places himself in the position of God-within, up inside Dre – possessing him and dissing him in the spirit of the hell that is 'the dark night of the soul' – and, when Tupac finally says, 'bless the real, all the rest get killed,' it's uncertain as to whether Dre will be the blessed or killed, as it's uncertain how Dre will emerge from his 'dark night.'

The other so-called 'disses' in the second verse of 'Toss It Up' can be read with equal amounts of ambiguity. 'Check your sexuality, as fruity as this Alize' can be interpreted as a diss from someone with a 'non-fruity' sexuality, or it can be read as a truth claim about the beginner on the path or even the Jungian Whole self as such, something to be marked, accepted, and moved beyond. The following lines certainly seem like Tupac is dissing Dre both for leaving Death Row Records and for leaving Compton:

> Lookin' for suckers 'cause you similar
> Pretendin' to be hard, oh my God, check your temperature
> Screamin' Compton, but you can't return, you ain't heard
> Brothers pissed 'cause you switched and escaped to the burbs.

Dre's a sucker or a parasite. He's pretending to be hard to make money when he's not. He can't return to Compton because the people there are mad that he made money and moved to the suburbs. Okay. These could be disses, but Tupac follows these lines by saying, 'Mob on this new era cause we untouchable,' and while the 'we' can be heard to refer to Tupac and Death Row Records, it can also be understood to refer to Tupac and Dre, as though Tupac says to Dre, with passion, conviction, and yet without judgment, 'You're a parasite who plays people. You act harder than you are to make money. You did well for yourself, and everyone's jealous of you for it. Move on. Mob on this new era. We can't be touched. Don't look back.' This line of reasoning is one of the main themes of Tupac's 'I Ain't Mad At Cha,' off *All Eyez On Me*, a track where Tupac clearly states to his impoverished brothers and sisters to do 'whatever it takes' to 'get up out the hood' and that, no matter what they do, he won't be mad at them. So why couldn't the same logic apply to 'Toss It Up?'

▲

Even though St. John of the Cross is unclear about what specific spiritual practices constitute the rituals of a beginner on the path of 'the dark night of the soul,' about to be schooled by God via a hellish purgation process, Vajrayana Buddhist texts, texts from its similar counterpart Chinese Taoism, and, for our argument, Tupac give hints to and positively value beginner practices, *up to a point*. (This doesn't imply that all beginner practices are completely moved beyond. From our understanding, frequently, they are not rejected once one ceases to be a beginner but are rather complicated, qualified, and combined with more advanced practices.) One of the most-referenced beginner practices is meditation-induced experiences of light and color.

Toward the end of the previous chapter focusing on Tupac and the skand(h)s, we looked at Plato's 'Cave Allegory' and the mistakes that can arise by not knowing one's own inner world of drives, memories, fantasies, and social conditioning as they pertain to vision. We also looked at the imperative to turn the lights off from St. John of the Cross. Here, we'll look at how Tupac maintains these motifs but complicates them to address meditation-induced experiences of light and color and the controversy surrounding the fact that they are beginner practices that constitute the experience of 'hell,' so to speak, as much as they comprise or lead one to what might be termed 'heaven.' In 'R U Still Down,' off the album *R U Still Down (Remember Me)*, Tupac states:

> Shit's gettin' sleazy, believe me
> Best to take what ya need, but don't be greedy
> Cause in my mind I see sunshine
> I thought
> I didn't have to run
> Now I'm duckin' from the gun yellin' 'One Time'
> Take your time to feel my record
> And if you did chill a second, my blind method will still wreck it.

When listening to these lines, it's difficult to determine where to begin each line because of how Tupac says 'I thought' and the timing he uses to say the phrase. Taken one way, you can place 'I thought' with 'I didn't have to run,' which makes sense. 'I thought I didn't have to run/ Now I'm duckin' from the gun.' However, as we mentioned, Tupac's pacing is off, so one can also hear Tupac saying, 'Cause in my mind I see sunshine, I thought.' Heard this way, we can interpret Tupac second-guessing the value of the light he saw in his mind or, if not second-guessing it, then just not seeing it anymore. Taken this way (which we'll explore), Tupac states that he thought he saw 'sunshine' in his mind, and the fact that he *thought* he saw sunshine highlights that there's something suspect about the figurative, internal light he once placed so much value on. However, it isn't as though he entirely discredits his inward gaze and experience with light, as he states that if one takes their time to 'feel his record,' or his whole experience, 'his blind method will still wreck it.' These statements complicate Tupac's position on the inward gaze and his experience with light-induced visualization. Seeing 'sunshine' in his mind is clearly something he thought was more than what it turned out to be, but, at the same time, he instructs listeners to take their time with the whole process, ending with what is ultimately a positive valuation of what he terms 'his blind method.'

Published in the journal *Frontiers in Psychology*, Lindhal, Kaplan, and Britton's "A Phenomenology of Meditation-induced Light

Experiences: Traditional Buddhist and Neurobiological Perspectives" argues, among several points, that the vastly documented experiences of light and color seen by Buddhist meditators are comparable to the experiences of those who have undergone perpetual isolation and sensory deprivation:

> Attenuation of sensory input reliably leads to hallucinations, even after a short time. Decreased sensory input leads to spontaneous firing and hallucinations through homeostatic plasticity – a set of feedback mechanisms that neuronal circuits use to maintain stable activity and firing rates close to a set point (Desai, 2003).

By removing input from the exterior world, the senses reveal their functionality and perceptions of the body itself. This research indicates that Buddhist meditation-induced experiences of light and color are comparable to perpetual isolation and sensory deprivation. It also suggests that they can awaken neuroplasticity or the brain's ability to rewire itself and create new neural connections.

> Whether through brain stimulation or sensory attenuation, changes in neuronal excitability that accelerate neuroplasticity can be used to facilitate therapeutic changes beyond usual training protocols.

These authors suggest that the meditation-induced light and color experience could open the mind and body to other functionalities. Yet, the authors also mark an array of Buddhist reactions to these light and color experiences; some texts suggesting that they are 'positive signs,' some framing them as 'involuntary side effects,' and others calling them 'imperfections' that can lead to 'distraction' and so should be ignored.

Vajrayana texts incorporate these practices into their heavy emphasis on mandala work. A trip to hell/ heaven, within a Judeo-Christian framework, comes by way of a deep, inner remembering of what was revealed to Adam and Eve – a daring to approach the orangish-red orb of fruit on the Tree of Knowledge, which, eventually, turns into the burning bush that states 'I Am That I Am', before helping Moses lead the Israelites out of slavery and then, finally, Christ's dictum 'I am the light of the world: he that followeth me shall not walk in darkness, but shall have the light of life.' For Taoists, it's woven into their accounts of alchemical transformation – a 'golden flower.' Literature addressing steps toward these experiences or reports of them play around a lot not only with figurations of the subtle body (the flows underpinning and interfusing the skandhas in the Buddhist tradition), but also – in some way, shape, or symbolic form – with figurations of the eyes, the chakras, and the erogenous zones. The infamous Taoist text *The Secret of the Golden Flower* is extremely elucidating about these connections.

Ever since Buddhism entered China in the third century BCE, Buddhism and Taoism have influenced one another. 'Tao' means 'the way' or flow of life, and, similar to Buddhism, passively surrendering oneself to the impermanence of the Tao is fundamental for Taoists in their quest to achieve harmony with existence. Or, more accurately, surrendering oneself to the Tao in a way that transcends the binary of passivity and activity is fundamental to achieving and re-achieving a forever-shifting balance between oneself and the world. Whenever we think about the complexity here, we think about surfing: apply too much active energy to the wave, and you'll sink into it; let the wave completely overpower you in your total passivity, and it will drown you. Thus, it takes something beyond activity and passivity to 'surf the Tao.' Attributed to Lu Dongbin of the late Tang dynasty, *The Secret of the Golden Flower* is a touchstone Taoist text on neidan or interior alchemy:

> Master Lu (Dongbin) said, the state of the Self is called Tao. The Tao has no name or form; it is just the essence, just the original spirit. Essence and life cannot be seen. They are contained in the light of heaven. The light of heaven cannot be seen. It is contained in the two eyes... The Golden Flower is light. ... [Chapter 1] The lower self is yin (feminine)... Refining the higher self [the masculine yang] is brought about by turning around the light, which is a means of preserving the spirit, a means of controlling the lower self, and a means of interrupting discriminating awareness... Just persist in this method, and naturally vitality-water will be sufficient, spirit-fire will ignite, intent-earth will stabilize and thus the holy embryo gestates. [Chapter 2]... Turning the light around is not just turning around the essence of one body, but turning around the very energy of creation. [Chapter 3].

As stated above, the Golden Flower or the light is not seen by the eyes but is contained inside of them. This motif of being unseen or only being able to be seen through an inward turn of the gaze is consistent in Tupac (something we just touched on previously). For example, in the track 'Can't C Me' off *All Eyez On Me*, funk superstar George Clinton states in the song's intro:

> The blind stares of a million pairs of eyes
> Lookin hard, but won't realize
> That they will never see the P
> You must be going blind.

The P, assumedly both Parliament (Clinton's infamous group), and Tupac – or Pac for short – standing in again for the God-within, will never be seen with blind or inwardly turned eyes because 'He' is that which is ever-changing and elusive. He is never still long enough to be 'seen' or known as a single entity. Yet, it is only by way of an inward turn of the gaze that this elusiveness can be approximated as an unknown or experienced in its evasiveness. Additionally, in 'Secretz of War' off *Still I Rise*, Tupac states,

> As I approach the scene, from smokin' green
> Got my eyes closed
> Niggas so cold on my foes
> I make 'em die froze
> Watch me make 'em bleed, make 'em Gs
> Lord help me wit' it
> Got me paintin' pictures of a meal ticket
> Help me get it.

The quality of what exactly Tupac is smoking (all inter alchemy can be figuratively represented as turning the body into a drug pipe) and the value judgment placed on the color green aside, Tupac is transparent here in stating that the foes he attacks are internal and that his manner of attack is one that is unleashed with his eyes closed, as is his visualization praxis wherein he sets his intentions: 'Got me paintin' pictures of a meal ticket/ Help me get it.'

In *The Secret of the Golden Flower*, a connection between the feminine lower self (yin) and the masculine higher self (yang) is achieved by 'turning around the light,' or rather turning around 'the very energy of creation' (possibly the same energy Alan Watts addresses in the quote from earlier on Kundalini/ Tantra methods), so that a kind of figurative self-pregnancy is achieved or a 'holy embryo' is allowed to 'gestate' (which, we have to mark, is slightly different from the notion of Buddha nature, which states not that an embryo has to be manufactured but that it is already there and that what has to be labored at is the removal of the defilements covering it up). This kind of virginal pregnancy of the unconscious can even be heard alluded to figuratively in 'Do For Love' off *R U Still Down*, when Tupac reappropriates the famous line from Sir Walter Scott's 'Marmion' as 'Oh what a tangled web we weave when we conspire to *conceive* (our italics),' conceive, here, simultaneously referencing both thinking and intercourse that leads to pregnancy. Conception. This redirection of flow that leads to a pregnancy that is unexplored or virginal comes about, according to *The Secret of the Golden Flower*, by using both the body and the eyes:

> The idea of focusing on *the tip of the nose* is very clever. The nose must serve the eyes as a guideline, but the nose itself is not the issue… Only when the eyelids are lowered properly halfway, is the tip of the nose seen in just the right way and therefore it is taken as a guideline. [Chapter 3]

By blocking out the periphery (or accessing a different kind of periphery) and focusing on the tip of the nose with eyes half-closed while using one's body to turn around 'the very energy of creation,' the mind's capacity to combine separate images captured by each eye to perceive depth is directed inward so that a vista opens onto that light which is internal.

This inner turn is what we understand Tupac to address in 'Heaven Ain't Hard 2 Find,' also off *All Eyez On Me*, from which we quote pertinent sections at length:

> I can see it clearly now
> Catch you smiling through your frown
> I'm askin' baby boo are you down…
> See it's all in your mind, so every time I sip a glass of wine I fantasize
>   until that ass is mine…
> This is a message to bomb bodies and all dimes
> Turn around one more time, heaven ain't hard to find…

> Heaven ain't hard to find
> In fact you can have it just have faith
> Just like a little kid, still believin' in magic…
> Touch me and let me activate your blood pressure
> This thug passion help the average man love better
> Picture me naked and glistening beneath the moonlight mist…
> Been talkin' since you arrived, but not a word is spoken
> Through my eye contact I wink and you respond back
> Lookin' mean, what's all that?…
> Oh God, help me, identify my truest thoughts
> Your hidden motives full of passion
> Who would have thought?…
> Until the end, it gets better with time
> I'm makin' love to your mind, baby
> Heaven ain't hard to find.

To begin to break these lyrics down to argue that Tupac is laying bare principles similar to those found in *The Secret of the Golden Flower*, we start with the simple observation that, like 'Toss It Up' (as well as many other Tupac songs), this track reads like a sex song, yet, at the same time, it not only explicitly presents itself as a map to heaven but also can be interpreted to addresses itself to God: 'Oh, God, help me identify my truest thoughts/ Your hidden motives full of passion/ Who would have thought?' The kind of 'intercourse' described in 'Heaven Ain't Hard 2 Find' is, according to Tupac, one where God can reveal to oneself either one's 'truest thoughts' or God's 'truest thoughts,' which, from a certain perspective, align. Moreover, Tupac clearly expresses sublime wonder regarding his discovery that God's secret plan for humanity hinges on 'passion': 'Your hidden motives full of passion/ Who would have thought?' We get it. For anyone who grew up under a conventional Christian upbringing, who would have expected this?

Tupac states several times that the 'intercourse' taking place in 'Heaven Ain't Hard 2 Find' is mental: 'See it's all in your mind, so every time I sip a glass of wine/ I fantasize until that ass is mine', and then again with the lyric 'Until the end, it gets better with time/ I'm makin' love to your mind, baby/ Heaven ain't hard to find.' But Tupac also lucidly states that what he's describing is not only spiritual and mental. Like popular forms of sex magic, it's also a practical tool for a better love life, and, let us be clear, this is love writ large. One of the biggest misconceptions about 'sex magic' (as certain spiritual practices are sometimes called in pop culture) is that it's exclusively about sex. It's not. So-called 'sex magic' (to speak generally because there are actually lots of different people who write in these terms with lots of different ideas) treats sex economy as a microcosm of all relations so that working on one's body and one's sexual relationship becomes a small-scale means to improve one's whole life:

> You can have it, just have faith
> Just like a little kid still believin' in magic
> …Touch me and let me activate your blood pressure
> This thug passion help the average man love better.

We understand Tupac's 'me' here to function in a similar way that his position in relationship to Dre functions in 'Toss It Up.' But, where in 'Toss It Up' Tupac takes the place of the God-within Dre, here, he positions himself inside of listeners themselves, who are figured as the female he's addressing.

This locationality is in keeping with the tradition we've already explored in texts like *Dark Night of the Soul* that represent practitioners as female bodies and God as a masculine spirit within; only here Tupac takes the place of God, and the listener takes the place of the female body being instructed by Him: 'Touch me and let me activate your blood pressure.' Considering that the whole track is about 'turning around' or turning back into oneself to access 'heaven,' we understand the 'me' Tupac says can be touched so that 'it' can activate one's blood pressure to be internal. This is all the more meaningful and perplexing when one considers the functionality of the senses. Meaning no listener ever really connects to Tupac's voice by way of external experience alone. A listener hears Tupac's voice coming across the speakers, it enters their ears, goes into their brain, and it's there, within the mind – inside of oneself – that listeners find Tupac, and not only does Tupac know this, but he goes out of his way to point it out to his listeners and build upon it. In this way, Tupac invites listeners to blur the boundaries between his voice as it's heard within his listeners' heads and his listeners' own thoughts, spirits, lights, or God-within. Tupac can 'see it clearly now' and 'catch' one 'smiling through their frown' because he speaks from that non-binary place that is underneath the surface of the skin, that place of inner light that always 'smiles,' shines, overflows, or exceeds oneself.

Repetition that points to the mechanics of turning around one's energy or turning inward abound in 'Heaven Ain't Hard 2 Find': 'Turn around one more time, heaven ain't hard to find.' While these lyrics highlight that heaven is to be found by way of a 'turning around' or turning back on oneself, the following lyrics underscore the role eye movement plays in the whole process:

> Been talkin' since you arrived, but not a word spoken
> Through my eye contact, I wink, and you respond back
> Lookin' mean, what's all that?

With the notion that Tupac repeatedly positions 'Heaven Ain't Hard 2 Find' as a roadmap to the heaven within, the body language (Been talkin'…but not a word spoken) Tupac describes above can be perceived to reference an internal dialogue that itself has a broad spectrum of implications.

The idea of having a conversation without 'a word spoken' can be taken to refer to an inner conversation of raw sounds as much as it can be taken to point out a more metaphorical internal dialogue between mind and body, between organs, between neural pathways, or between the channels of the subtle body. Conversation, in this context, just means exchange. In 'Heaven Ain't Hard 2 Find,' we interpret the winking 'eye contact' to point out something similar to the focusing of one's half-closed eyes onto the tip of their nose from *The Secret of the Golden Flower* – essentially a reversal of depth perception that evokes a back-and-forth play between the eyes and what *The Secret of the Golden Flower* terms 'the light that is contained' inside of them. Something comparable to rapid eye movement therapy or EMDR (eye movement desensitization and reprocessing) but with one's eyes mostly closed. The line 'Through my eye contact' can itself be understood to underscore the contact point between the eyes and the light contained within the eyes. The image Tupac evokes here is one of a face-to-face exchange between one's own face turned backward in an inner gaze and the light-eyes-face within (the face that embodies the light contained within the eyes). Similar to how Tupac can 'see it clearly now' and 'catch' one 'smiling through their frown,' when Tupac, from an internal vantage point as the face of light within, winks, and one, with their gaze reversed, responds back 'lookin mean,' he proceeds to exceed and press one's mean face into its own opposite. Playfully, flirtatiously, he states, 'Lookin' mean, what's all that?' – the implication being that his positive energy is about to, like the other lyrics suggest, overwhelm the face's frown into a smile.

In 'Heaven Ain't Hard 2 Find,' Tupac frames the discovery of the God-within by way of beginner methods as a joyous discovery that, although it may be off-putting at first, is ultimately sacred and sexual at the same time. This, however, isn't always the case. Tupac frequently posits the self-reflexive moment of coming face to face with one's own veiled otherness as a negative, terrifying moment or as a moment of imprisonment. In the track 'Cradle to the Grave,' off *Thug Life*, Tupac states, 'Are you scared of the dark?/ Can't close my eyes I see visions,' and he sometimes frames the same 'wink and response' play between the eyes and the light contained inside them as a violently revolutionary attack – where the winking eyes become a kind of machine gun turret fire (or dueling Glocks or switch-hitting punches) directed against egocentrism and the restrictive structural formations within. This is the situation with 'Holla At Me,' also off *All Eyez On Me*, which must be contextualized before we can show how it figures the 'wink and response' theme as a kind of inner, political insurgence. 'Holla At Me' cautions against being trapped by the 'evil' of 'money.' Tupac repeatedly says throughout the track that since he's the 'type of nigga, that let the evil of the money trap' him, that people should 'holla at him' or help keep him in check. Yet, at the same time, Tupac also positions himself in the track as the one who 'hollas' at or calls out others who are trapped by the evils of money. 'Money' may seem like a straightforward and literal signifier. Yet, within the tradition of 'the game' of individuation or enlightenment, it can also symbolize the flows that comprise or interact with what is sometimes called 'the subtle body.'

Jewish mysticism – similar to other esoteric traditions we've been exploring here, like Vajrayana Buddhism and Taoist alchemy – describes a body-centric enlightenment program or, at least, an enlightenment program that must pass through the body to reach enlightenment. *Kabbalah* methods also schematize a pathway to 'God' in terms of a sexual union between the male and female aspects of oneself and between oneself and one's sexual partner. Jewish mysticism, at times, also frames the 'turning' about of energies described by Taoism as a money transfer from the masculine to the feminine. (We briefly touched on this idea in the chapter on Tupac's sacred biotech when looking at how in South Asia semen is figured monetarily, but we will address it further, or from a different angle, here.) Written in the 13th Century in Spain, the *Zohar* is the touchstone text for Jewish mystics or Kabbalists. Written by Moses de Leon and ascribed to the work of hermit-rabbi Shimon bar Yochai, among several of its objectives, the *Zohar* reflects upon and interprets the 613 Commandments of the *Torah*. The portion that thinks through commandment nine is what interests us here:

> The ninth commandment: to be generous to the poor and provide them with food, for it is written: *Let us make a human being in our image, according to our likeness* (Genesis 1:26). *Let us make a human being* – jointly, including male and female; *in our image* – the wealthy; *according to our likeness* – mystery of the poor. For the wealthy derive from the side of the male, the poor from the side of the female. Just as they constitute a single partnership – one caring for the other, providing for the other, and rendering goodness – so should human beings below be rich and poor in a single bond, one providing for the other and rendering goodness.

The ninth commandment – to be generous to the poor – works in three ways: (1) it requires that literally wealthy people care for the poor, (2) it demands that actual men care for their wives, and (3) it not only deems necessary that the masculine side of oneself transfers subtle-body wealth to one's feminine side but also requests that one employs that capital to figuratively impregnate or produce a being within ('Let us make a human being in our image'). Translator and commentator of the Stanford University edition of the *Zohar Volume 1,* Dr. Daniel C. Matt, says the following in a footnote regarding the above phrase '*in our image* – the wealthy': 'Our *image* indicates *Tif'eret*, who transmits the rich flow of emanation to *Shekhinah, our likeness,* who 'has nothing at all of Her own." Tif'eret and Shekhinah are sephirot or chakra points on the Kabbalah Tree of Life – a Jewish mystic map of the subtle body. As in Taoism (opposite other traditions like Vajrayana Buddhism), where yin is associated with the moon that absorbs and reflects the light of yang, Kabbalah's feminine side, called Shekhinah, absorbs and reflects the light of the masculine Yesod, and Tif'eret (the heart or gut region) acts as an intermediary that transfers 'the rich flow of emanation,' which in the above quote is figured in monetary terms, from the wealthy male side of self to the wanting female side.

So, by reading 'Holla At Me' through a Kabbalist lens, we're able to frame the danger of being trapped by money as the danger of the solidification of the skandhas that then block the subtle body or the threat of one's body being imprisoned by the repressive policing apparatus of one's own ego ideal. We explored this phenomenon in great detail in the chapter in this book dealing with the Buddhist notion of skandhas and Freud's account of the ego ideal, the skandhas being closely aligned with the subtle body, and the ego ideal being that internal policing apparatus that crystalizes in the mind when the skandhas become rigid. Furthermore, we developed the idea that the ego ideal or inner voice and image of normalization can be figured as something like financial currency – especially in a congealed (and not in a liquid) form – due to the notion that a dangerous ego ideal, spawned from repression, is the miserly accumulation of the skandhas. More still, anticipating feminist critiques of how the feminine aspect of self is depicted as lacking in the above quote from the *Zohar*, we've already established that if 'she's' lacking in Tupac it's the result of one's own (or society's) violence against her. Whether this is the case in the *Zohar* itself is a detour we can't embark on at this time. We can say with confidence, however, that Shekhinah (the feminine aspect of both God and self) is a massive source of sacred power in that system.

Belittling someone who's gotten themselves stuck in a beginner's hell for turning their back on him, 'Tupac' – again taking the position of the God-within – says in 'Holla At Me,' 'You could never be live until you die/ See the mothafuckin' bitch in your eye.' We've quoted this line previously. However, we want to look at it again from a different angle. Before, we focused on the figure of 'death' and how the enlightenment process is sometimes framed as a death/ rebirth. Now, within the context of that play between the eyes and the light contained within them described in *The Secret of the Golden Flower*, we refocus on this line through a new lens. Or, rather, we build on our previous point. In one sense, we recognize that this line is probably popularly interpreted straightforwardly – Tupac literally wishes death upon someone because they're 'a bitch' or they're weak, and this can be seen in their eyes. In another sense, however, we understand Tupac to mark in this line that the pathway to death/ rebirth begins by turning one's attention to the feminized light within the eye – associated with what Jung terms the anima in its shadow form, the veiled feminine spirit within in its wrathful manifestation. In this way, we understand the line as an imperative, almost like a magic incantation or prayer, that the person Tupac is attacking turn their gaze inward – in order to be 'live,' one must 'die,' and, in order to 'die,' it's requisite that one first see the 'bitch' in one's eye. In yet another way, we also recognize that the tradition of talking about the anima negatively or marking 'her' wrathful, 'bitch' aspects is well documented, and we underscore again that what Tupac describes here are beginner methods that are designed to exacerbate the illusory hell one already lives in so as to lead one through that place to a better way of life. 'Turn your gaze inward,' we interpret Tupac as saying, 'and see your inner feminine self so that you can make your peace with her lest, instead of living with femininity, you wind up living with a bitch.'

Tupac even goes so far, in one instance, to explicitly gender God as feminine. In 'Blasphemy,' off *Makaveli*, Tupac says,

> We probably in hell already
> Our dumb asses not knowin
> Everybody kissin ass to go to heaven ain't goin'
> ... Niggas in Jerusalem waitin' for signs
> God's comin' she's just takin' her time
> Ha ha.

Here, we get several ideas we've been exploring corroborated: (1) the idea that hell and heaven are experienced on earth, (2) the idea that God can be feminine, and (3) the notion that this feminine God is tricky and aggressive or 'a bitch,' in other words, the notion that she makes you wait for her to arrive and, in one sense, might not ever arrive ('God's comin' she's just takin' her time'), which, we suggest, is partially why Tupac ends this line with laughter.

'The King of Tantras, the Glorious Mahamaya,' from the Vajrayana tradition, describes Mahamaya – the secret goddess-like dakini within – thusly:

> She [the dakini] is their great secret, the great Queen Mahamaya. She is the great illusion, intensely fierce, who destroys all that exists.

The sacred, inner feminine here is paradoxically described both as an illusion and as the destroyer of illusions, the illusion that annihilates illusions. Similar to our analysis of 'Skandalouz' in the first chapter, where the shadow-anima (shadowy because it reflects the blocked skandhas, and so, in a certain regard, is fake) presents herself as the scandalous trickster who teaches one how to overcome her, the dakini is both illusion and the destroyer of illusions. And this destructive capacity or wrathful capacity of the inner feminine is also shown in 'Blasphemy.' In *Kabbalah*, instead of addressing the one anima or dakini as having both wrathful and peaceful aspects, the Jewish mystics talk about different females within. Lilith, for example, (who is to be discovered within), is said to be the evil first wife of Adam who tries to use his seed to spawn demons. Lilith (associated with the beginner's experience) precedes Eve, and both Lilith and Eve are shadowy echoes of Shekinah (who has the most feminized power in that system, if not the most power altogether). The lines that follow those already quoted from 'Blasphemy' are

> Livin' by the Nile where the water flows
> I'm contemplating plots, wondering which door to go
> Brothers getting shot, coming back resurrected
> It's that raw shit, nigga check it.

Since these lines follow those prior ('God's comin' she's just taking her time'), the inference can be made that it is this goddess-like spirit within (now figured as the entire mythic milieu of the flowing Nile, surrounded by sacred doors), who, after making one wait and wait, arrives only to spontaneously shoot one down before bringing them back from the dead. This, we suggest, is the other reason Tupac laughs after stating, 'Niggas in Jerusalem waitin' for signs/ God's comin' she's just taking her time/ Ha ha.' She – according to both Tupac and the esoteric, spiritual tradition we've been exploring – doesn't just arrive on a cloud, ready to dole out hugs. If she comes (and hopefully either one figures out how to avoid her wrath or she does in fact come), she comes to assassinate oneself or the egocentric aspect of oneself.

In 'Holla At Me' and elsewhere, Tupac represents the play between the eyes and the light-eye-face within as a criminal, revolutionary attack meant to violently dismantle rigid power structures inside oneself. This debatably 'criminal' backward gaze, within traditions frequently drawn upon by the black community, is seen depicted in the famous symbol of the Sankofa Bird from the Akan tribe in Ghana.

According to the Carter G. Woodson Center (Carter G. Woodson is the 20th century intellectual most famous for founding 'Negro History Week,' an earlier version of 'Black History Month'), '[T]he literal translation of the word and the symbol is *'It is not taboo to fetch what is at risk of being left behind.'*' It also translates as 'to go back and get.' What is often overlooked in readings of the Sankofa Bird is the word 'taboo' in this phrase. Typically, the Sankofa Bird is understood to symbolize the importance of the mental exercise of going back into history (represented by the world egg depicted in the bird's mouth) to reclaim significant achievements or rescue erased stories to use them to help forge a better tomorrow. The word 'taboo,' however, suggests that there is potentially something transgressive or 'criminal' invoked in the backward gaze of the Sankofa Bird – but possibly also an exceptional, paradoxical kind of criminality that is simultaneously forbidden and permitted – and that it might refer to practices similar to what the Buddhists, Taoists, and Tupac describe. The phrase 'It is not taboo' to go back and retrieve 'what is at risk of being left behind' just ends up highlighting that whatever process of reclamation the symbol evokes (which we suggest is what we've been calling the inward turn) presents as taboo. Why would you have to bother to tell someone that something wasn't taboo unless there was a possibility of them seeing it that way? And, you know, it's worth considering that maybe it is.

The criminality of the backward gaze is clearly articulated in 'Holla At Me' when Tupac addresses his 'criminal elevation,'

> No hesitation
> This information got you contemplatin'
> Heartbreakin' and eliminatin' with the conversation
> Break him and let him see the face of a mental patient
> It's a celebration of my criminal elevation.

The evil of 'money' not only has the person Tupac addresses in his discourse trapped, but it has him conflicted to the point where he's 'contemplatin'/ Heartbreakin' and eliminatin' with the conversation' or shattering the internal dialogue between oneself and one's own.... What do we call this? Who is being conversed with? If we are to believe St. John of The Cross, who says that both God and the Deceiver, posing as God, speak to one during the dark night of the soul, it all gets pretty blurry. Is one conversing with the Devil, with one's own inner policing apparatus that reinforces rigid structures of conformity and obedience within the body, the masculine 'him' in the phrase 'Break him?' Or does the 'him' here refer to God? Or both? Tupac positions himself in this track as that which will be freed once the 'conversation' between oneself and one's inner police officer/ God is shattered, as 'breaking' this conversation is a 'criminal' activity that leads to Tupac's celebration-worthy 'elevation' out of the inner depths of repression. Moreover, Tupac is clear in stating that the way to 'heartbreak' and to 'eliminate' this repressive internal dialogue or rigid-skandha 'money trap' is to let one's internal police officer/ God see 'the face of a mental patient.'

We understand this 'criminal' manifestation of a mental patient's face described in 'Holla At Me' to be a violent and revolutionary figuration of the play between the eyes and the light within (or the light behind each eye, the light-eye-face) mentioned in *The Secret of the Golden Flower*. The 'face of a mental patient' is the rapid-fire 'wink' and 'responding back' that dismantles the rigid icon of the dictator within. In *A Thousand*

Plateaus: Capitalism and Schizophrenia, French philosopher Gilles Deleuze and French psychoanalyst Felix Guattari playfully figure the kinds of meditation-induced experiences of light and color that Buddhists and Taoists describe as a ruining of the rigidly structured face of the tyrant/ deity within. Destroying the light-eye-face means to

> no longer look into the eyes, but to swim through them, to close your eyes, to close your own eyes, and make your body a beam of light moving at an ever-increasing speed.

Interestingly here, we see a bit of the paradox that circulates around both the imperative for one to close their eyes and to open them, as Deleuze and Guattari state that one is to 'close' one's 'eyes' and then clarify that they are to close one's 'own eyes.' This implies (taken one way) that the eyes belonging to the self are the eyes conventionally understood (one's literal eyes) and that by closing one's 'regular eyes' the light eyes described in Taoism then open, suggesting that so long as one's literal eyes remain open Taoism's eyes of light within remain closed. But, seeing as how the eyes of light represent something like one's 'true self' or 'non-self,' the reverse interpretation can also be put forth. It's all quite schizophrenic. Furthermore, the schizophrenic, for Deleuze and Guattari, is potentially both figuratively and literally a properly radicalized, psychotic agent capable of taking down oppressive social institutions and rigid identity formations. Tupac, like Deleuze and Guattari, advises students to let their inner police officer 'see the face of a mental patient.' This is what promises to bring about figurative death and liberation for Tupac, as he says to the person he addresses in 'Holla At Me,'

> Probably never knew the way it feels to die
> So you figure, fuck with me, I'll give that ass a try
> Nigga holla at me.

For Tupac, there are clear parallels between the experience of God, backdoor channels, death, and madness.

To combat the routinization of samsara – a Buddhist term referring to the world of suffering, the world of constant back-and-forth clinging that occurs between binary opposites like life and death or happiness and sorrow – Tupac states that his 'only fear of death is reincarnation' and that he's 'bustin' on his adversaries like a mental patient' in 'Ballad of a Dead Soldier' off *Until the End of Time.* In 'Life of an Outlaw,' off *Makaveli,* Tupac says, 'Merciless madman, screamin' kamikaze in tongues/ Automatic gunfire makin' all my enemies run.' This breakdown of the formations that hold words and sound structures within bounded space, which is also figuratively 'suicidal' – this 'screamin' kamikaze in tongues' – is a religious experience for Tupac. Recall that, similarly, in the Christian tradition, Pentecost is the celebration of the day the Holy Spirit descends on Jesus' disciples, and, in some interpretations, it is said to speak to them in tongues or to cause them to speak in tongues – that point where language forms rupture into raw sound potential. Similarly, listeners/ practitioners are said to tremble before Tupac in sublime fear when they encounter him in 'Hell For a Hustler' from *Still I Rise,* trembling being another breakdown of form. A blurry body gone erratic. Yet, Tupac also makes it clear here that, even though he references the power of insanity in tracks like 'Holla At Me' and 'Life of an Outlaw,' insanity is not his endgame and should not be the goal of his students:

> No insanity plea for me
> I ride the beef 'til I burn
> Censor me and bar your kids from the lessons I learned
> And, in turn, I'm hostile. Guess you could call me antisocial
> Niggas shakin' like they caught the Holy Ghost when I approach 'em.

As with the bodhisattva tradition, the ecstasy of God is beyond words and descriptions – effectively 'crazy wisdom' or madness that doesn't get lost in the beyond but rather leads to sanity. The work of the spiritual student is to push through this moment of being 'caught' by 'the Holy Ghost' and take the position that one will not plead 'insanity' but will rather learn from it and incorporate its revolutionary knowledge into everyday life. This is extremely difficult physical, emotional, and mental work that, in the end, leads to practicality, on the one hand, and revolutionary strategy, on the other.

Whether for good or ill, the lesson of learning how to relinquish one's egocentrism – that part of oneself that doesn't recognize that it is connected to everything and so mistakenly thinks of itself as separate, propertizing, and accumulating – is ultimately what Tupac emphasizes in his multiple references to this inward turn of the gaze. No one articulates this lesson of using the internal gaze to shatter one's egomania more beautifully than the 19th-century American philosopher Ralph Waldo Emerson, who, like Tupac, was inspired by Christianity (or Christ rather) and Hinduism. In the essay "Nature," Emerson says the following about the eye:

> There is a property in the horizon which no man has but he whose eye can integrate all the parts, that is, the poet... The sun illuminates only the eye of the man, but shines into the eye and the heart of the child. The lover of nature is he whose inward and outward senses are still truly adjusted to each other; who has retained the spirit of infancy even into the era of manhood... In the woods, we return to reason and faith... Standing on the bare ground, – my head bathed by the blithe air, and uplifted into infinite space, – all mean egotism vanishes. I become a transparent eye-ball; I am nothing; I see all; the currents of the Universal Being circulate through me; I am part or particle of God.

For Emerson, the eye doesn't respect property lines. It takes in all yet owns nothing. This gaze or glance is especially for those poets who hold onto their inner child because, as Emerson states, 'their inward and outward senses are still truly adjusted to each other.' In other words, the eye here is both an external and an internal gaze or glance. To go into 'nature,' for Emerson, is to go into the nature within as much as it is to go into the wilderness without. It's in this boundaryless nature that Emerson describes one being able to lose their egocentrism and become invisible, become 'a transparent eye-ball' without an 'I' that, by seeing itself as everything and by allowing all of nature to pass through it, annihilates its separateness.

Tupac corroborates and furthers Emerson's lesson on using the eye to lose the 'I' in 'Unconditional Love' off his posthumous *Greatest Hits* album. 'Unconditional Love' switches between being about a mother's love, the love of friendship, and the love for self, but in all instances, references to the eye persist and are what interest us here. Tupac states in the song's chorus:

> In this game the lesson's in your eyes to see
> Though things change, the future's still inside of me
> We must remember that tomorrow comes after the dark
> So you will always be in my heart, with unconditional love.

Unconditional love is, by definition, like Emerson states, egoless. To give love and receive love without conditions means that nothing is owed by either party. Debt does not exist. It is non-transactional. It is a pure gift, desire driven not by lack but excess. There's always more than enough to give. For Tupac, even though he is dealing with the 'game' of enlightenment and its corresponding levels, the gift of the 'lesson' is in the 'eyes to see.' From our understanding, this means that both the lesson itself and what it produces are gifts. The future is a constant present that exists 'inside' of oneself, in an inside that is always fracturing illusion so it can be clearly revealed that the inside is the outside flowing through oneself just as what is within is constantly being released without.

Not only is the 'tomorrow' that 'comes after the dark' the reward, but the 'remembering' that 'tomorrow comes after the dark' – a remembering of a tomorrow that both occurs within and lives inside the present moment – is a reward unto itself. The gift is the loss of boundaries separating inside from outside, the condition of always having others in one's heart and always being within the hearts of others – a total loss of self. As *The Secret of the Golden Flower* states, this gift is not found in what the eyes can capture and possess but in what is already always living inside of them, which can never be owned or controlled and, furthermore, which will always be in the process of leaving oneself. It is the eternal pregnancy that is always emergent and overflowing, not only always arriving but also always taking its leave. As Tupac states in 'Unconditional Love':

> I'll probably never understand your ways
> With everyday I swear I hear ya
> Trying to change your ways while gettin' paid at the same time
> Just had a baby with the same eyes
> Something inside, please let me die
> These are strange times
> How come I never made it
> Maybe it's the way I played it in my heart
> I knew that one day I gotta be a star

> My hopes and all my wishes
> So many vivid pictures, and all the currency I'll never even get to see
> This fast life soon shatters
> Cause after all the lights and screams
> Nothing but my dreams matter.

While having 'a baby with the same eyes' can literally mean producing an offspring that has eyes similar to one's own, given the tradition we've highlighted (which we know Tupac studied with the utmost seriousness), like in *The Secret of the Golden Flower*, one can also use one's eyes to gestate a sacred embryo within, or, as with Buddha nature, uncover the embryo that was always present. As *Kabbalah* makes known, 'trying to change' one's ways 'while gettin'' paid at the same time' can also describe the strange and sacred redistribution of inner wealth or the individuation process of enlightenment that underscores a counterintuitive, shocking, and confounding longing to die in order to be reborn into the light or to be reborn 'a star.'

The gift of unconditional love is that even though everything 'shatters' in the end that is also the beginning, the persistence of dreams and the act of dreaming remains, for better or for worse. It is the labor of trying to stay in this presence that Tupac address in 'Only Fear of Death' when he states, 'my only fear of death is reincarnation.' This is a fundamental Buddhist goal, the goal of nirvana. Nirvana isn't heaven. It's the absence of heaven and hell, freedom from the closed loop of samsara or the wheel of suffering that circles back from death to life, happiness to sorrow. This is why Chogyam Trungpa maintains that before taking up the Tantric path, one must not only be familiar with Mahayana and Theravada Buddhism first, but one must also surrender to a complete and utter sense of hopelessness:

> Hope is a promise. It is a visionary idea of some kind of glory, some kind of victory, something colorful... As long as we possess a body and our face, our face and our façade, we have no chance at all of being liberated, none whatsoever. It is as hopeless as that. There is no hope, absolutely no hope. We are going to be drawn into, and drowned in, a deep pool of shit, an ocean of shit, that is bubbling, gray in color, but smelly at the same time.

When Tupac says in 'R U Still Down?', 'It seems I can't find my focus, and, homie, I ain't paranoid/ I've seen the future and it's hopeless,' he does so with an authentic understanding of the workings of samsara. Understanding samsara is about pattern recognition: If darkness always follows light and death always follows life, one can see the future or predict that this pattern will permeate everything. Once this prediction is made, one can begin to reorient themselves to reality accordingly. This is the hopelessness that Chogyam Trungpa and Tupac speak of. Enlightenment can't happen until one understands this endless repetition thoroughly, and, as Tupac says:

> This fast life soon shatters
> Cause after all the lights and screams
> Nothing but my dreams matter.

For Tupac, there is no victory, nor is there defeat. There is no dreamer, and there is no dream. There is only the ongoing business of dreaming. The dream is all that matters or materializes ad infinitum. And even though 'the future' is 'hopeless' for Tupac, the real mystery for him comes through the fact that there is love in this disconsolate world. This he makes clear in 'Holler At Me' when he says:

> Trust, a no no
> Love is a mystery. Fuck the po po
> Holler at me.

For Tupac, the real gaping gulf of Love that one staggers before – utterly stupefied – only emerges after one moves beyond trust and attacks, first and foremost, their internal policing apparatus. Only once this agent of inner oppression has been put into check will Love reveal themselves. And then one will have the remainder of their life to not only ponder how it's possible that Love exists at all, but one will have the rest of their life to do their best to follow Love's example. 'Holler at me.' 'Holler if you hear me.' If you have eyes to see, then see. If you have ears to hear, then hear.

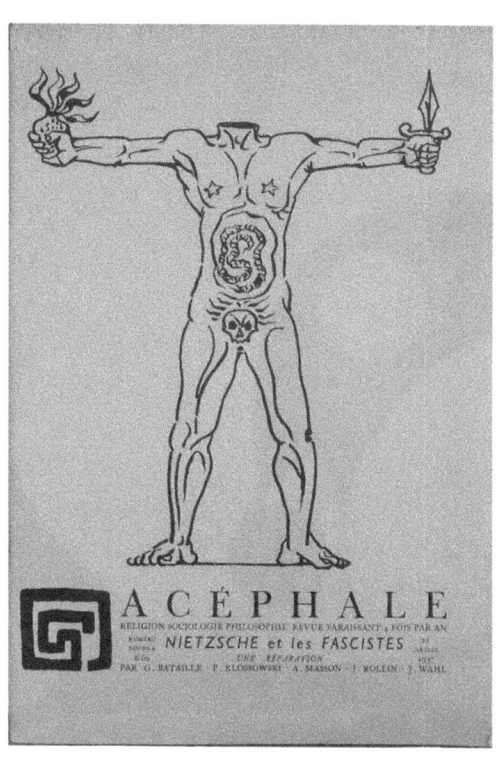

The Acephale secret society (above).
Georges Bataille (below).

Sankofa Bird, Ghana.

MEDIA, CINEMA, FEMINISM and CULTURAL STUDIES

J.R.R. Tolkien: The Books, The Films, The Whole Cultural Phenomenon
J.R.R. Tolkien: Pocket Guide
The *Lord of the Rings* Movies: Pocket Guide
The Cinema of Hayao Miyazaki
Hayao Miyazaki: *Princess Mononoke*: Pocket Movie Guide
Hayao Miyazaki: *Spirited Away*: Pocket Movie Guide
Tim Burton : Hallowe'en For Hollywood
Ken Russell
Ken Russell: *Tommy*: Pocket Movie Guide
The Ghost Dance: The Origins of Religion
The Peyote Cult
Cixous, Irigaray, Kristeva: The *Jouissance* of French Feminism
Julia Kristeva: Art, Love, Melancholy, Philosophy, Semiotics and Psychoanalysis
Luce Irigaray: Lips, Kissing, and the Politics of Sexual Difference
Hélene Cixous I Love You: The *Jouissance* of Writing
Andrea Dworkin
'Cosmo Woman': The World of Women's Magazines
Women in Pop Music
HomeGround: The Kate Bush Anthology
Discovering the Goddess (Geoffrey Ashe)
The Poetry of Cinema
The Sacred Cinema of Andrei Tarkovsky
Andrei Tarkovsky: Pocket Guide
Andrei Tarkovsky: *Mirror*: Pocket Movie Guide
Andrei Tarkovsky: *The Sacrifice*: Pocket Movie Guide
Walerian Borowczyk: Cinema of Erotic Dreams
Jean-Luc Godard: The Passion of Cinema
Jean-Luc Godard: *Hail Mary*: Pocket Movie Guide
Jean-Luc Godard: *Contempt*: Pocket Movie Guide
Jean-Luc Godard: *Pierrot le Fou*: Pocket Movie Guide
John Hughes and Eighties Cinema
Ferris Bueller's Day Off: Pocket Movie Guide
Jean-Luc Godard: Pocket Guide
The Cinema of Richard Linklater
Liv Tyler: Star In Ascendance
Blade Runner and the Films of Philip K. Dick
Paul Bowles and Bernardo Bertolucci
Media Hell: Radio, TV and the Press
An Open Letter to the BBC
Detonation Britain: Nuclear War in the UK
Feminism and Shakespeare
Wild Zones: Pornography, Art and Feminism
Sex in Art: Pornography and Pleasure in Painting and Sculpture
Sexing Hardy: Thomas Hardy and Feminism

The Light Eternal is a model monograph, an exemplary job. The subject matter of the book is beautifully organised and dead on beam. (Lawrence Durrell)
It is amazing for me to see my work treated with such passion and respect. (Andrea Dworkin)

CRESCENT MOON PUBLISHING
P.O. Box 1312, Maidstone, Kent, ME14 5XU, Great Britain. www.crmoon.com

cresmopub@yahoo.co.uk   www.crescentmoon.org.uk

www.ingramcontent.com/pod-product-compliance
Lightning Source LLC
Chambersburg PA
CBHW060538100426
42743CB00009B/1569